Making Inclusion Happen

Anne Hayward is a leading expert in the fields of inclusion and special educational needs (SEN) in schools, colleges, Children's Services and charities. She has been the DfES consultant for learning support units, learning mentors, the Excellence in Cities programme and for the SEN and Disability Team on Special Schools and Specialist Status.

With a background as a teacher, headteacher, Senior LEA Inspector, OFSTED Registered Inspector, FEFC Inspector and a Deputy Director of Education, Anne has over twenty-five years' experience of SEN and inclusion, and has developed a wealth of knowledge and practical materials.

Anne works in a host of mainstream and special schools, support services and colleges. Hence her philosophy on inclusion, 'Making It Happen', is rooted in experience and practical application.

Anne is an accomplished trainer with a truly down to earth and practical approach to making things work on the gound. She runs training courses across the country for managers, school staff and multidisciplinary professionals on inclusion and working with young people with mental health problems, challenging and difficult behaviours.

Anne has a really useful website www.annehayward.com which contains a range of practical materials that can be used in schools and elsewhere.

MAKING INCLUSION HAPPEN

A Practical Guide

Anne Hayward

P·C·P

Paul Chapman
Publishing

First published 2006

 Paul Chapman Publishing
A SAGE Publications Company
1 Oliver's Yard
55 City Road
London EC1Y 1SP

SAGE Publications Inc
2455 Teller Road
Thousand Oaks, California 91320

SAGE Publications India Pvt Ltd
B-42, Panchsheel Enclave
Post Box 4109
New Delhi 110 017

Library of Congress Control Number: 2005910370

A catalogue record for this book is available from the
British Library

ISBN-10 1-4129-2221-6   ISBN-13 978-1-4129-2221-0
ISBN-10 1-4129-2222-4   ISBN-13 978-1-4129-2222-7 (pbk)

Typeset by C&M Digitals (P) Ltd, Chennai, India
Printed in Great Britain by The Cromwell Press, Trowbridge, Wiltshire
Printed on paper from sustainable resources

CONTENTS

Contents of accompanying CD   vi

Acknowledgements   viii

How to use this book   ix

1   The National Inclusion Agenda   1

2   Inclusion Programmes and Initiatives   15

3   Developing an Inclusive School   41

4   Managers and Management Matters   67

5   Self-Evaluation – Measuring the Impact   85

6   Maximising Your Resources   101

And Finally ... Managing Change Effectively (Without Losing the Plot)   112

Glossary   115

Useful Books   117

Index   119

ACCOMPANYING CD

How to Use the CD

The CD contains PDF files, labelled 'Worksheets.pdf' which contain worksheets for each session in this resource. You will need Acrobat Reader version 3 or higher to view and print these pages.

The document is set up to print to A4 but you can enlarge them to A3 by increasing the output percentage at the point of printing using the page set-up settings for your printer.

CHAPTER 1 – CD EXAMPLES

- Barriers to learning (Example 1)

CHAPTER 2 – CD EXAMPLES

- Protocol for managed moves (Example 1)

- Factors which have contributed to the success of the LSU and a plan of the LSU (Example 2a–b)

- Example of primary school learning mentor action plan (Example 3)

CHAPTER 3 – CD EXAMPLES

- Building Design – considerations to be made when planning the area campuses as inclusive learning environments (Example 1)

- Examples of inclusion policies/statements (Example 2a–b)

- Inclusion policy self-evaluation checklist (Example 3)

- Inclusion action plan (Example 4)

- Inclusion referral systems (Example 5a–b)

- Checklist for schools – key features of an inclusive school (Example 6)

CHAPTER 4 – CD EXAMPLES

- In tray exercises for interviews (Example 1)

- Pupil inclusion indicators (Example 2)

- Pupil behaviour review checklist (Example 3)

- Example checklist for pupil file (Example 4)

- Example of a common meeting format (Example 5)

CHAPTER 5 – CD EXAMPLES

- PowerPoint slides on self-evaluation (Example 1)

- Case study template (Example 2)

- School behaviour review plan (Example 3)

- Self-audits – pupil mobility (Example 4)

CHAPTER 6 – CD EXAMPLES

- Social inclusion of costed action plan (Example 1)

- Blank cost of provision in year (Example 2)

- Example of inclusion database (Example 3)

ACKNOWLEDGEMENTS

The inspiration for this book comes from the wonderful schools, agencies, local authorities, staff and pupils that I have worked with over the years. The dedication to the spirit of learning and true devotion in ensuring that young people get the education they so richly deserve spurred me on during hard times. I have such admiration for staff at the grass-root level, Learning Mentors, Teaching Assistants, teachers and multi-agency staff who undergo a roller-coaster of emotions in a single day!

Thanks to my secretary, Sue Fisher, for her unstinting support, good humour and patience, Sue Collins for keeping us fed during very tense times … her lemon mousse is second to none, Suzanne Mitchell for reading the manuscript and generally keeping me to task and, lastly but not least, my husband Richard for his care and thoughtfulness in putting up with my strops!

I would also like to thank the following for granting permission to use their work in this book and CD: Enfield Local Authority, Maltby School in Rotherham, Broadgate Primary school in Leeds, Anne Fowlie, West Drayton Primary School in Hillingdon, Rush Croft Sports College in Waltham Forest, Burnage High School in Manchester, Foxhill Primary School in Sheffield, Springwood Heath Primary school in Liverpool, Vicky Moss from Sheffield Local Authority, the Educational Psychology Service in Rotherham, Birmingham BIP, Longdendale Community Language College in Tameside, Liz Vicary from Tower Hamlets Local Authority, Milton Keynes Local Authority, Linda Disney from Bradford Local Authority, Bristol Local Authority and others who very kindly shared their wonderful practice. There is a wealth of practical material on my website www.annehayward.com which will complement this book.

HOW TO USE THIS BOOK

The inclusion agenda is highly complex and is evolving all the time. It is very easy to become overwhelmed by the volume of information and initiatives. This book aims to help anyone involved in delivering inclusive services to find their way through the maze, understand the really important issues and then translate these into effective practice.

The idea for the book came from a course I have been running very successfully all over the UK. It has a similar title to this book 'Making it real … Making it happen!' The course is based on my many years of experience in the inclusion field and a comprehensive knowledge of what is going on in schools and agencies. In my work as consultant to the DfES, I have visited mainstream and Special Schools across the country and have collated enormous amounts of best practice. I also work as Advisor on Inclusion to the Romanian government and train teachers over there.

I developed my inclusion course in order to share my knowledge, experience and the best practice that is going on all around the UK. This book has the same objective. It aims to provide a succinct overview of the current inclusion agenda and legislation (no mean feat). It looks at a wide range of programmes and initiatives and how they can be used to support young people with a wide range of barriers to learning. I look at how to move towards an inclusive school and how to get it right first time, including developing an inclusion strategy and policy, inclusion models and the practical management issues around inclusion.

There is advice on self-evaluation and how to put in effective systems which will help you ensure ongoing improvement and provide the evidence for the Self-Evaluation Form, as required under the new Office for Standards in Education (OFSTED) inspection framework. There is also guidance on maximising your resources, effective procurement and managing change.

Within the chapters, I include 'Suggestions for making it happen' – these are practical tips to help you implement inclusion effectively without losing the plot. At the end of each chapter, there is a section called 'Look it up' which signposts you to further useful sources of information and websites.

The CD which accompanies this book has useful examples of best practice. Further examples of training resources and materials for staff, governors and other agencies can also be found on www.annehayward.com. Why reinvent the wheel when there is so much good work going on out there?

Although English case studies have been used they are equally applicable to Ireland, Scotland and Wales. The barriers to learning across the United Kingdom are complex and reflect the specific context of the school and local communities, however the strategies to meet those needs will be similar and complementary.

Web Adresses:

Wales
www.wales.gov.uk
www.learning.wales.gov.uk
Scotland
www.ltscotland.org.uk/inclusiveeducation/
www.hmie.gov.uk
www.parentzonescotland.gov.uk

Throughout this book, I hope to give anyone involved in the inclusion field the confidence to understand the current agenda and make informed choices about the best provision in their particular context or setting. In this way, young people will be able to access the best support for their needs and to fulfil their potential. Above all, I hope to inspire you by showing just what can be achieved with the right approach, drive and commitment.

CHAPTER 1

The National Inclusion Agenda

Inclusion is an increasingly important part of the government's agenda and it is committed to ensuring that all pupils are integrated as far as possible into the daily life of schools and the local community. This chapter aims to provide a succinct overview of the national context for inclusion and to help schools and other agencies develop a clear understanding of the current agenda, including the most recent *Every Child Matters* and Children's Services legislation. Clearly, the context is changing constantly and it is important to keep up to date – guidance is provided on useful sources of information. It is essential that everyone who is involved in inclusion familiarises themselves with the latest national context, as this will form the basis for inclusion services (and, indeed, inspections) in the future. This chapter guides you through the maze and helps you focus on what really matters. It also signposts you to other sources of useful information.

A background to inclusion

Inclusion has historically focused on the issue of special educational needs (SEN) within schools and local authorities (LAs). Services and support have been provided via a special needs co-ordinator (SENCO) within schools for pupils with a range of specific, identifiable needs such as:

- learning difficulties
- a physical disability
- hearing or visual impairment
- speech and language difficulties
- significant behavioural and emotional needs
- those who have profound and complex needs.

Those young people with significant, complex needs have places at Special Schools through the statementing process. Pupils with any other difficulties such as attendance, disaffection and mental health problems have traditionally been the responsibility of pastoral staff in schools.

In 2002, the Department for Education and Skills (DfES) set out the principles for an inclusive education service:

- Inclusion is a process by which schools, local authorities and others develop their cultures, policies and practices to include all pupils.

- With the right training, strategies and support nearly all children with special educational needs can be successfully included in mainstream education.

- An inclusive education service offers excellence and choice and incorporates the views of parents and children.

- The interests of all pupils must be safeguarded.

- Schools, local authorities and others should actively seek to remove barriers to learning and participation.

- All children should have access to an appropriate education that affords them the opportunity to achieve their personal potential.

- Mainstream education will not always be right for every child all of the time. Equally just because mainstream education may not be right at a particular stage, it does not prevent the child from being included successfully at a later stage (*Inclusive Schooling – Children with Special Educational Needs* – DfES, 2002).

In more recent years, the inclusion agenda and context has shifted from pupils with SEN to those with the full range of *barriers to learning* including:

- disaffection

- mental health issues

- ethnicity and cultural issues

- transition and pupils who move frequently

- gender

- human rights issues

- learning difficulties

- significant challenging behaviour

- young carers

- pupils from a community which has a disregard for education

- unstable family circumstances

- attendance and punctuality issues

- drug-dependent young people.

There is now a much wider recognition that schools and other agencies need to take a much more holistic approach to meeting the varying needs of pupils, depending on the latter's individual circumstances. The result has been that SEN is now set in a much wider context and encompasses a far greater range of barriers to learning. Considerable extra resources have been made available to many schools to promote more effective inclusion for pupils with a greater range of barriers to learning, with a concentration of additional funding into inner city schools and those within challenging areas. This includes funding for programmes such as Excellence in Cities, Behaviour Improvement Programmes and New Deal for Communities. Although funding to schools and school budgets will change in terms of schools having more control over their budgets. Many of these funding programmes will still be allocated to schools through their designated school budget. This expansion of the inclusion agenda has led to a wider range of staff and services now being provided within mainstream schools along with new approaches to integrating pupils. This includes:

■ the introduction of new staff into schools, for example learning mentors, learning support unit staff, inclusion managers, therapists, counsellors and Connexions personal advisers. As a result of which, many schools, particularly secondary, are developing multi-agency, multi-professional teams and structures

■ introducing more flexibility into the curriculum

■ introducing new teaching methods, which meet the needs of a range of learning styles

■ the development of appropriate, differentiated learning materials.

A useful exercise to introduce this concept of inclusion to staff and governors is to list the range of barriers to learning that are in the school and get staff to discuss the implications for assessment and management within the curriculum and their classrooms. Figure 1.1 is a very useful checklist to use with staff and governors to get them thinking about the range of barriers to learning in school. There will be additional barriers which will be identified by them, which you can add as part of the exercise. Figure 1.1 is also on the CD, Chapter 1 Example 1, so you can extend and change the format to suit your context.

Attainment		
Barrier/potential bar	**Assessed by/from**	**Desirable outcome/success criteria**
Poor literacy skills	KS 2/3 SATS	Performance in line with potential
Poor numeracy skills	KS 2/3 SATS	Performance in line with potential
Underperformance against potential	CATs/MINDYIS score	Performance in line with potential
EAL	Personal records and attainment	Performance in line with expectation
		(Continued)

Attendance		
Barrier/potential bar	**Assessed by/from**	**Desirable outcome/success criteria**
Poor attendance	Register	Full attendance and achievement in line with potential
Young carer	School records	Support from appropriate agencies achievement in line with potential
Long-term sickness	Register/personal record	Maintaining good progress on individual learning plan
Punctuality	Observations/late book	Reduction and strategies in place to encourage better attendance

Disaffection and reduce exclusions		
Barrier/potential bar	**Assessed by/from**	**Desirable outcome/success criteria**
Disaffection	Referral: school records; inappropriate behaviour	Behaviour conducive to learning Achievement in line with potential
In danger of exclusion History of exclusion	School record behaviour	Achievement in line with expectation: behaviour conducive to learning

- **Improve motivation to learning**
- **Reduce bullying**
- **To raise standards for underachieving groups**
- **(Any of the above due to deprivation/social factors)**

Barrier/potential bar	Assessed by/from	Desirable outcome/success criteria
Victim of bullying	Referral: records	Incidents resolved: raise self-esteem; performance in line with expectation
Unstable/difficult family circumstances	Personal records: LAC records	Support from appropriate agencies: performance in line with expectation
Looked after students (students in public care)	Records	Enhance communication with social services: achievement in line with expectation
Low self-esteem vulnerable	Referrals from staff, carers: personal records; child protection register	Raise self-esteem, confidence. friends/peer support; performance in line with potential
Several school changes	Personal record	Performance in line with potential
Refugee mobility	Records	Identification of need: appropriate support; performance in line with potential
Cultural disregard for education	Records: parental involvement; extra-curricular	Engagement in process: performance in line with potential
Drugs and alcohol related	Records/observations	Multi-agency teams in place to address needs and reduce dependency
Curriculum	Performance in subject areas	Improved attainment and good progress made
Attitude and culture in school	Feedback/observation	Development of positive and inclusive cultures

Figure 1.1   Excellence in Cities – barriers to learning

The Special Educational Needs and Disability Act 2001 provides a statutory framework for inclusion. It strengthens the right of children with SEN to attend a mainstream school, unless their parents choose otherwise or if this is incompatible with 'efficient education for other children' and there are no 'reasonable steps' (Special Educational Needs and Disability Act – DfES, 2001) which the school and LA can take to prevent that incompatibility. Alongside that Act, the Disability Discrimination Act 2001 (DDA) places new duties on schools not to treat disabled pupils less favourably than others and to make 'reasonable adjustments' (Disability Discrimination Act 2001) to ensure that they are not disadvantaged. The new legislation expects mainstream schools to include all pupils fully, making appropriate changes to their organisation, curriculum, accommodation and teaching methods. It places duties on schools and LAs to ensure this happens.

A revised *SEN Code of Practice* took effect in 2002. The revised code sets out five principles:

- that children with SEN should have their needs met

- that their needs will normally be met in mainstream schools

- that the views of children should be sought and taken into account

- that parents have a vital role to play in supporting their children's education

- that children with SEN should be offered full access to a broad, balanced and relevant curriculum in the Foundation Stage and later years.

The Code highlighted very clearly the need for the statementing process to fall within strict time limits, and the roles and responsibilities of the LA, schools, voluntary sector and the independent parental supporter. Details of these time limits can be found within the *SEN Code of Practice* and on the DfES website www.DfES.gov.uk.

In 2003, the DfES reviewed the role of Special Schools. The DfES Ministerial Working Party on the Future of Special Schools recommended that Special Schools should:

- be outward-looking centres of expertise and work more collaboratively with mainstream schools

- increasingly cater for the growing population of children and young people with severe and complex special educational needs

- go through the process of change in terms of leadership, teaching and learning, funding and structures

- develop the way in which they work with the National Health Service, Social Services and other agencies which provide support beyond the classroom.

Special Schools are a great source of expertise and specialist resources but they are having to take increasingly complex pupils who demand higher levels of resources. Many Special Schools have developed a comprehensive outreach support service, particularly to meet the needs of pupils with physical, learning, communication, emotional and behavioural difficulties. Because mainstream schools are now integrating a much wider range of needs, if inclusion is to work effectively, schools need access to a greater range of staff expertise. This can be developed from within the school staff or can be bought in as appropriate under a Service Level Agreement (SLA) from

Special Schools or other specialist agencies. It is therefore essential that there is meaningful dialogue between mainstream and Special Schools and agencies. Excellent partnership working can then be developed in which both the pupils and staff benefit. The South West SEN Regional Partnership has produced two very good practical handbooks on developing effective outreach mainstream and special schools. These can be found on www.sw-special.co.uk.

The DfES *Strategy for SEN Removing Barriers to Achievement* in 2004 sets out the government's vision for SEN over the next ten years and priorities for the future through four key areas:

- early intervention

- removing barriers to learning

- raising expectations and achievement

- delivering improvements through partnership.

There are 11 SEN Regional Partnerships in England with a brief which involves looking at broader inclusion issues but with a strong focus on SEN. The national priorities for the regional partnerships are:

- developing more inclusive policies and practice

- improving efficiency and effectiveness of SEN processes and services

- responding to and engaging effectively with government initiatives

- improving inter-agency working.

This has resulted in training, and conferences on inclusion, being the prioritised activities of all 11 partnerships. Details of their work and publications can be found on www.teachernet.gov.uk.

The inclusion agenda brings together all the services and support for young people under one umbrella, encompassing the full range of barriers to learning. It takes a holistic approach to meeting pupils' needs and recognises, for example, that if a pupil has a problem at home, this can affect learning at school. Taking a joined-up approach to meet a child's needs is key to the concept of inclusion.

Children's Services agenda

The government paper *Every Child Matters*, which is now the basis for the Children Act 2004, aims to improve opportunities and outcomes for children, young people and families. This legislation is central to making inclusion happen in schools. Key elements include:

- building services around the child, young person and families to achieve improved outcomes

- understanding and responding to children's needs in a holistic way

- supporting parents, carers and families

- better safeguards for children and young people

- focusing on opportunities for all and narrowing the gaps

- developing the workforce and changing culture and practice

- integrating working practices, processes, strategy and governance.

Every Child Matters outlines five key outcomes for children:

- *Be healthy.*

- *Stay safe.*

- *Enjoy and achieve.*

- *Make a positive contribution.*

- *Achieve economic well-being.*

These five key outcomes now form the basis for the structures of the Children's Services departments in local authorities and for future OFSTED inspections.

There will be an increased emphasis on *personalised learning* and pupil-centred learning processes: this complements the emphasis on individual pupil programmes with the learner at its heart through flexible curriculum packages, range of learner support strategies and individualised programmes so that each pupil can reach his or her potential.

Multi-agency working

The Children's Services agenda has significant implications for local authorities – the Children Act 2004 forms the basis of a long-term programme of change in the way Children's Services work together. Local authorities are required to change their structures for education, health and social services in line with the new legislation and establish Children's Services Departments with a director responsible for all these functions.

Authorities will need to develop Children's Trust arrangements to integrate front-line services. Children's Trusts will work together with local partners from the private, public, voluntary and community sectors to assess local needs, agree priorities and commission local services to meet these priorities. From April 2006, these will be reflected in a new Children and Young People Plan that brings together all local authority planning for children and young people.

The Act places a duty on local authorities to promote co-operation and sharing of information between agencies in order to maximise achievement of the five key outcomes. It creates an integrated inspection framework and Joint Area Reviews (JARs) to assess the progress of local areas in improving outcomes.

Good information-sharing is the key to successful collaborative working along with early intervention to help children and young people at risk of poor outcomes. Information-sharing will be a key feature that will be assessed by children's services inspections. All local authorities will be developing information-sharing databases into which education, health and social services will input key information about individual children. In each local authority there will be an Information Sharing and Assessment Team, which will be a central source of information for all those involved in inclusion within that area.

The Common Assessment Framework (CAF) is currently being developed and local authorities are expected to implement this between April 2006 and the end of 2008. It is a nationally standardised approach to conducting an assessment of the needs of a child or young person. It is particularly suitable for use in education, health and social services to identify and tackle problems before they become serious. Hopefully, this should streamline relationships between schools and other services and help practitioners undertake assessments in a more consistent way. Where the assessment indicates that the child has urgent or complex needs requiring specialist input or assessment, the CAF will feed into the next part of the assessment process.

One of the key features of *Every Child Matters* is the need for clear, planned collaborative work between agencies around the preventative agenda. The next few years will see an extensive reconfiguration of services to offer earlier, more coherent, support which meets the needs of children and families in local settings in a more streamlined way. A web-based toolkit to support the delivery of multi-agency working in schools and early years settings has been published by the Every Child Matters: Change for Children programme.

There is no single correct way of multi-agency working. The DfES, through a review of practice, shows that it is possible to group multi-agency working into three broad models. These models are intended to assist schools and other agencies to think through their structures.

The DfES describes the three models as:

1. *Multi-agency panel*

    (a) Practitioners remain employed by their agency.

    (b) They meet as a panel or network on a regular basis to discuss children with additional needs who would benefit from multi-agency input.

    (c) In some panels, casework is carried out by panel members. Other panels take a more strategic role, employing key workers to lead on casework.

    An example of this type of working arrangement is a Youth Inclusion and Support Panel (YISP).

2. *Multi-agency team*

    (a) A more formal configuration than a panel, with practitioners seconded or recruited into the team.

    (b) The team has a leader and works to a common purpose and common goals.

    (c) Practitioners may maintain links with their home agencies through supervision and training.

    (d) There is scope to engage in work with universal services and at a range of levels – not just with individual children and young people, but also small group, family and whole-school work.

Examples include Behaviour and Education Support Teams (BESTs) and Youth Offending Teams (YOTs).

3. *Integrated service*

    (a) A range of separate services that shares a common location, and works together in a collaborative way.

    (b) A visible service hub for the community.

    (c) Has a management structure that facilitates integrated working.

    (d) Commitment by partner providers to fund/facilitate integrated service delivery.

    (e) Usually delivered from school/early years setting.

    Examples include Sure Start children's centres and Extended Schools that offer access to a range of integrated, multi-agency services.

One of the challenges in multi-agency working is the common understanding/use of language and terminology. In all organisations, including schools, there can be an overreliance on jargon and acronyms. With the greater involvement of other agencies and their jargon, this can compound the problems of communication and understanding between different professionals. This is particularly the case when many of the professionals are coming from differing backgrounds and have job titles that are new to many working in schools. Recently, at a multi-agency conference in the North West of England with a wide range of different professionals attending, the delegates were asked to define their understanding of the word 'assessment' and 45 different interpretations were received. Therefore it is important to establish and agree a common understanding around language and terminology. A glossary has been produced by the DfES to help this process along as part of the multi-agency web-based tool kit. This can be accessed from www.everychildmatters.gov.uk/multiagencyworking.

Multi-agency working is a key element of the Children Act and therefore the inclusion agenda. It will be the cornerstone of the Inclusion Policy and Strategy in schools and within local partnerships of schools and agencies. Another challenge will be to co-ordinate the professionals and range of work undertaken with the child or young person and the family/carer. In reviewing service provision, local authorities will work with their partners to develop new roles such as that of 'lead professional' to ensure that there is a joined-up approach to service provision for pupils with a range of barriers to learning and additional needs. A lead professional may come from the school or partner agency, whichever is more appropriate. The key functions of this post are described in Chapter 4.

There will need to be a clear mapping of provision, particularly for those children with additional/special needs. Services will have to be commissioned, quality systems established and the integrated inspection framework implemented to monitor progress and quality. All of this requires effective and co-ordinated strategic planning at all levels, including the involvement of all agencies and users. Gaps in provision and staff skills will need to be identified and considerable training and development put in place.

New Relationship with Schools

Within education services there will be a New Relationship with Schools (NRWS). The aim is to help schools raise standards – with clearer priorities, less bureaucracy, greater accountability and better information for parents. The government is to increase legal and financial flexibility for schools alongside the introduction of a more streamlined accountability regime. Schools will become more autonomous and funding will be fully devolved from 2006, with little ring-fenced funding. This will impact on the school's inclusion budget as, before this, much of the funding for SEN and Excellence in Cities (learning mentors/learning support units/gifted and talented) was ring-fenced; now it will go into the global school budget. In effect, the inclusion manager will need to make a case to support the needs of pupils in the school alongside other interests and priorities. Chapter 6 outlines these changes and looks at ways to make the case for Inclusion funding, whilst ensuring services meet best value requirements.

Key elements of the NRWS include:

- Changes in the inspection process with smaller, more focused inspections based on a Self-Evaluation Framework (SEF) and the five outcomes. Chapter 5 outlines this in more detail.

- School funding will change to three-year funding and an overall Dedicated Schools Grant (DSG) which will incorporate money from existing funding streams.

- External support moving away from link advisers to nationally accredited School Improvement Partners (SIP).

- Emphasis on school self-evaluation as a starting point for all internal and external monitoring/evaluation.

- Alignment of data and communication into a 'single conversation'.

There are a number of models being piloted in terms of partnerships, learning networks and funding methodology. The dissemination of funds to local areas and local decision-making structures is a key feature of this strategy. Each local and geographical area will interpret and develop practice in varying ways. Networking will be important in order that practice is shared and developed, particularly within the inclusion agenda.

School Workforce Remodelling/Agenda for Change

This government programme involves remodelling roles in schools in order that teachers can focus on teaching and learning in the classroom rather than other administrative or pastoral roles. Extra salary points in England will be given to teachers for teaching and learning rather than other tasks. Schools will make greater use of other professionals such as higher-level teaching assistants, learning mentors, personal advisers, pastoral support workers and so on. These roles will feature across the inclusion provision in removing barriers to learning. Chapter 4 has more details about these various roles and how they will all work together. Schools will need to publish their new management structure by January 2006 and have it implemented by 2008. The Inclusion Team is likely to be the largest staffed, and have the greatest variety of roles within it.

Alongside this remodelling is the Children's Workforce Strategy which is based on the five *Every Child Matters* outcomes and aims to develop a workforce that is skilled, well managed and supported by effective, shared multi-agency systems. The strategy has four key strategic challenges:

- Recruit more high-quality staff into the children's workforce.

- Retain people in the workforce by offering better development and career progression.

- Strengthen inter-agency and multidisciplinary working.

- Promote stronger leadership and management.

The DfES Children's Workforce Unit is currently developing guidance in all areas around the Children Act and, in particular, training. There is more information on inclusion training in Chapter 3.

Extended Schools Programme

The Extended Schools Programme expects schools to provide a core offer of extended services either on site or across a cluster of local schools and providers. In essence this means after-school resources will be placed in schools to extend their provision. In primary schools these will include services such as study support activities, sports, arts, homework clubs, parenting support opportunities including family learning, swift and easy referral to a range of specialised support services and childcare available from at least 8 a.m. to 6 p.m. term time and school holidays. Secondary schools would have in addition a 'youth offer' which would consist of a range of before and after school holiday activities to engage young people and the opening up of information and communications technology (ICT), sports and arts facilities to be used by the wider community.

Early years

At the early years level, the government intends to put in place a joined-up system of support from pregnancy onwards through the National Service Framework for Children, Young People and Maternity Services (NSF), an integral part of the *Every Child Matters* programme. Over the next ten years existing provision will be integrated and expanded to provide parents with a range of accessible, high-quality and affordable options for early learning and childcare. The Sure Start programme will be extended, with a view to 2,500 Sure Start children's centres operating by 2008. The DfES's new early years and childcare strategy – Choice for Parents, the Best Start for Children: A Ten Year Strategy for Childcare – aims to improve access to quality childcare, often within schools and/or in partnership with the voluntary and private sector. Consultation is currently under way and the subsequent Childcare Bill, expected to be in place by 2008, will give parents the right to accessible and high-quality childcare and early years provision. In addition, the DfES's Five-year Strategy for Children and Learners sets out an expectation that primary schools should, over time and perhaps working in partnerships, offer childcare 48 weeks a year between 8.00 a.m. and 6.00 p.m. More details can be found about the strategy on www.DfES.gov.uk.

Suggestions for making it happen ...

- The inclusion agenda is wide and varied and needs to be understood by everyone involved in meeting pupil needs. The Inclusion Team need to brainstorm ideas about informing all staff with respect to the varied needs of pupils.

- Inclusion is a process and is not developed overnight. The Inclusion Team will need to develop a clear time plan for developing greater inclusive activities over the forthcoming year. This information will need to be integrated into the school Self-Evaluation Form (SEF).

- Schools will need to allocate sufficient resources and staffing to meet the huge range of pupils' needs coming through which must be identified and assessed. As these pupils require a more flexible approach to the curriculum and other aspects of school life all staff will be required to review their policies and practices.

- As not all pupils' needs will be met in mainstream schools, close links should be made with local authority officers, Special Schools, statutory and voluntary groups and services both locally and regionally.

- There needs to be a strong emphasis on training for all staff within school and from outside agencies.

Youth Green Paper

In addition to the *Every Child Matters* legislation and guidance, the DfES published a Green Paper, *Youth Matters*, in 2005. This has the aim of improving collaborative working between all those who work with young people to provide them with the best possible support. The paper recognises that most young people cope well with their teenage years, which are an important period of transition bringing many challenges. However, some young people have significant difficulties during this phase including disaffection, drugs, teenage pregnancies, anti-social behaviour or crime.

The Green Paper sets out for consultation a new strategy for supporting all young people, with an emphasis on those who are vulnerable or at risk. The vision for the strategy mirrors that of *Every Child Matters* (ECM) – ensuring that all young people can meet their full potential by focusing on the same five outcomes as ECM and organising services around the needs and aspirations of young people. The Green Paper proposes devolving responsibility and resources for providing young people's services to local authorities, working through Children's Trusts, schools and colleges, to other key partners and to young people themselves. The current Connexions service will be integrated with a wider range of services at local level.

The reforms proposed in the Green Paper will need to be completed by April 2008.

Further education agenda

Mainstream sector colleges play a significant part in continuing the inclusion provision for students with learning disabilities and difficulties (LDD). Many will provide 'taster' courses for students with LDD from 14 years and all should provide courses and a range of opportunities for students from 16 years. Many will have courses at National Vocational Qualification (NVQ) level 1 in a number of vocational areas as well as alternative provision such as Award Scheme Development and Accreditation Network (ASDAN) and Open College Network. In addition there will be work training providers who will deliver opportunities for students with a range of difficulties to develop work and employment skills. This provision in England is funded mainly by the Learning Skills Council; in Scotland, Wales and Northern Ireland there will be similar bodies to undertake this process.

Many colleges will have an inclusion manager or a manager for students with LDD. There will also be provision for those students with specific literacy/numeracy/basic skill difficulties and many have support for those students who exhibit behavioural and emotional issues. Colleges have to comply with the DDA and have to produce audits and plans for improvement. Currently the guidance that colleges follow in terms of the quality and range of provision is under consultation and the Little Report, due out in Spring 2006, should provide a basis of good practice around the country.

For those students with more profound and specialist needs, there are independent specialist colleges. These are funded by a range of bodies including the Learning Skills Council, local authorities, health and social services. At present the Connexions service co-ordinates placements to these colleges and mainstream sector colleges. Future strategy in these areas will be to work towards placing students in their local areas and communities rather than outside the borough. Therefore some mainstream sector colleges are developing greater specialist provision to meet the needs of the more highly dependent and complex students.

Suggestions for making it happen ...

■ Make sure everyone in your organisation familiarises themselves with this agenda so you are all clear about the big picture. The inclusion agenda will permeate through all the work you do and you need to get your head around it. There needs to be an understanding of the agenda throughout your organisation, particularly among key decision makers, including school governors.

■ Why not ask each member of the team to research a particular part of the national legislation? Then come together as a team and share what you have learned. In this way, you will all become familiar with the agenda without the burden falling on the shoulders of one person.

■ Hold briefings for everyone in the organisation to ensure a clear understanding of the inclusion agenda and to start the debate about the implications for the organisation.

■ Establish a resource bank of useful materials for reference by the whole organisation. Give a member of staff the task of keeping everything up to date.

■ Develop an issues paper which looks at the impact the inclusion agenda is likely to have on your organisation. This will get you thinking about what you need to do. The practical guidance in the following chapters will help you actually do it.

Look it up ...

- Children Act 2004 and *Every Child Matters*: fact sheets www.dfes.gov.uk

- Consulting on new school funding arrangements from 2006–07 and New Relationship with Schools: Next Steps, www.teachernet.gov.uk/publications

- DfES *SEN Code of Practice 2002*, Special Educational Needs and Disability Act 2001, Disability Discrimination Act, Removing Barriers to Achievement DfES Strategy for SEN 2004, www.dfes.gov.uk

- Details of different agencies and their statutory remit and the function of the various agencies including schools under the Children Act, and a range of *Every Child Matters* initiatives, www.everychildmatters.gov.uk

- Developments and practical guidance from the Children's Workforce Unit, www.every childmatters.gov.uk/deliveringservices/workforcereform

CHAPTER 2

Inclusion Programmes and Initiatives

This chapter broadens the inclusion agenda and shows the huge expansion of programmes and initiatives that have been put in place in recent years. It provides an overview of the SEN statutory requirements, to which all schools and agencies working with children with special needs are required to adhere. It looks at the practical issues which schools and other agencies face around the wider inclusion agenda, particularly in relation to the broader range of barriers to learning such as behaviour, attendance and mental health. There is an overview of a range of key initiatives and programmes which have been developed over the past few years to address these needs.

SEN legislation and framework

In order to provide equality of opportunity, fulfil the inclusion agenda and to help all children achieve a high standard and reach their full potential, the government introduced the Special Educational Needs and Disability Act in 2001. This Act, linked to a revised *SEN Code of Practice*, took effect from January 2002.

The Act strengthened the right to mainstream education for children who have statements, and sought to enable more children with special educational needs to be successfully included in mainstream education. Equally, where a parent wants a place at a Special School, their wishes should be taken into account. The new statutory framework for inclusion requires that:

- pupils with SEN, but without a statement, must be educated in mainstream schools except in exceptional circumstances

- pupils who have a statement must be educated in a mainstream school unless this is against the wishes of the child's parents or is incompatible with the provision of efficient education for other children.

Recent educational developments such as greater autonomy for schools over their budgets and approaches to delivering the curriculum and the emphasis on results and standards have created a dilemma for SEN and the inclusion agenda. While wishing to fulfil the statutory framework and educate pupils with SEN in mainstream schools, some schools are finding it difficult to come to terms with producing high academic results and educating pupils with a wide range of ability, some of whom will not contribute, in the school's view, to the standards agenda. It is important for school leadership teams and inclusion staff to:

- ensure that the school's admission criteria and practices do not discriminate against pupils with SEN or other barriers to learning

- spend time informing governors of the range of need coming into the school and the positive impact that has on ethos, attitude, pupil experience, and range of curriculum and accreditation on offer

- work closely with parents of pupils with SEN ensuring that they fully understand the needs of their child and the steps that the school is making to support them. All parents should be made aware of the range of pupil need in the school and the positive impact that this can have for all. However, information on how the school is approaching SEN, in particular behaviour and discipline, needs to be very clear as this is usually a contentious issue for many parents.

The following principles and values are inherent in providing a quality education for pupils with SEN and useful for the school to use in a leaflet/information sheet for parents/carers:

- Pupils are valued equally.

- They make progress.

- There is a close working partnership between parents/carers and children.

- Needs are identified and assessed as early as possible, and are met as soon as practicable.

- Pupils should have access to a relevant, broad and balanced curriculum.

- There is close liaison between the SENCO/appropriate member of the inclusion team and the parents.

The *SEN Code of Practice* provides practical advice to schools and other settings in carrying out their statutory duties to identify, assess and make provision for children's special educational needs. Separate guidance, *Inclusive Schooling – Children with Special Educational Needs, DfES, 2002*, provides practical advice on the statutory framework for inclusion. A *Disability Rights Code of Practice for School*s, prepared by the Disability Rights Commission, will explain the new anti-discrimination duties to schools and help them plan strategically and make progress in:

- improving accessibility for disabled pupils to school premises and to the curriculum

- improving the delivery of written information in an accessible way.

The SEN Code outlines the stages that schools should put into place for identifying and assessing need, and the plans that must be written, reviewed and monitored. There are three stages:

1. **School action** – the various strategies and support that are available within the classroom and the school.

2. **School action plus** – will involve outside agencies.

3. **Statementing** – this is when considerable outside assistance is required. An alternative placement may also be considered owing to the level of need.

In organising support for pupils at these three levels, schools and the Inclusion Team in particular will need to have:

■ effective administration and pupil filing systems

■ clear identification of need strategies and support/guidance for classroom and subject staff in using them

■ commitment from all staff to adapt/differentiate the curriculum at school action

■ a system of review to ensure that pupils are at the right stage and that the support that they need is appropriate

■ protocols that ensure any outside or internal support at school action plus is of quality and meeting pupil and school needs

■ a whole-school database which records the level and type of support for each pupil (this is outlined in Chapter 5).

Statements are the culmination of various reports from professionals working with the child and contributions from the parent and child. There are clear time limits for making assessments, and procedures that need to be followed. This can be a time-consuming and administratively burdensome process but it is essential that there is a key member of staff, usually the SENCO, who is monitoring this process and keeping track of time limits and ensuring that the pupil and family are not disadvantaged. The local authority will have a range of support services helping families through this process. The school will need to give the parent information about these services. Statemented pupils have a legal right to the level of provision and placement that is on the statement and schools have a responsibility to ensure that the pupils' needs are met. In the past it was the parents who asked for the assessment leading to a statement, now the school can request the assessment. It is very powerful if the school's request for a statement is supported by the parents. Parents who are not happy with the statement and its recommendations can appeal to the independent Special Educational Needs and Disability Tribunal (SENDIST) to have their case heard, and they have the right to see the local authority response. There appears to have been a rise in the number of appeals to the tribunals over the past few years. The implications for schools are as follows:

■ Ensure that there is evidence of good working relationships with the parents, evidence needs to be tracked and audited as the tribunal will request this information.

■ The tribunal will have a copy of the school's SEN/inclusion policy so the school needs to make sure that there is evidence of the policy in practice with regard to the case.

■ That parents have been involved in the setting of their child's targets and Individual Education Plans (IEPs). There should be documented evidence, such as reports, correspondence through email and letters, showing that they have been involved and have worked closely with the school over their child's provision.

Once a statement is in place, it must be reviewed at least on an annual basis, and individual education plans written to set targets and measure progress. If there are problems arising with the provision, schools must not hesitate to bring forward any review. Some schools, and in my experience primary schools in particular, keep some pupils who have significant difficulties in school for too long as it may seem a failure to admit that something is not working. In reality the pupil's needs may have changed, and the capacity of the school to meet these may not be sufficient.

Suggestions for making it happen ...

- Ensure that everyone is fully familiar with the SEN statutory framework.

- Ensure there is an up-to-date SEN policy and nominated governor for SEN, although schools need to start appointing a governor for inclusion in recognition of the changing agenda.

- Ensure that all pupils with SEN, at School Action, School Action Plus and Statement stage have individual or other relevant plans in place that are reviewed regularly, and that the resources and support are co-ordinated effectively.

- Put in place a DDA audit and plans to meet the legislative requirements.

- Develop strategies to include parents more effectively in their child's education.

- Develop closer links with local Special Schools/units/services for pupils with Social, emotional and behavioral difficulties (SEBD) and mental health difficulties.

- Forge links with the regional SEN Partnership to inform strategic planning and gain access to resources. Look at the website www.teachernet.gov.uk/wholeschool/sen/regional

The wider inclusion agenda

In 2004 OFSTED produced a report, *Special Educational Needs and Disability – Towards Inclusive Schools,* which looked at the extent to which the vision of inclusion is becoming a reality in schools. One of its main findings was that 'The admission and retention of pupils with social and behavioural difficulties continue to test the inclusion policies of schools'.

With the widening inclusion agenda, the government has put resources into a range of support through programmes such as Excellence in Cities (EiC) and Behaviour Improvement Programmes (BIP) which aim to develop differing roles to support those pupils with a wide range of barriers to learning. In the book *Emotional Health and Well Being – a Practical Guide for Schools*, it states:

> In any school of 1,000 pupils there are likely to be 50 pupils with a depressive illness, 100 who are suffering significant distress, 10–20 with obsessive compulsive disorders, 6–10 girls with an eating disorder; of the rest a large number will have less serious problems which nonetheless affect their well being.

Clearly, these factors have considerable implications for schools and the way in which schools deal with these difficulties has a significant impact on the outcome for the young person.

Behaviour management in schools

Managing pupils with challenging and problematic behaviour is a key aspect of the inclusion agenda which tests most schools. Much has been written about behaviour and behaviour management, but it really comes down to the ability of staff and the capacity of schools to put policies into practice in a consistent way. Over the past six years there has been a plethora of guidance from the DfES, and a wide range of programmes and initiatives from which all schools can benefit. The challenge is 'seeing the wood for the trees', picking up key essential points and seeing them through via a whole-school agenda.

In December 2002, the Secretary of State launched a national behaviour and attendance programme: this comprises universal and targeted elements. All secondary schools have now been provided with audit and training materials and consultancy support as part of the behaviour and attendance strand of the Secondary National Strategy. A comparable behaviour and attendance strand of the Primary Strategy including curriculum and training materials is being piloted in 25 local authorities. The Social and Emotional Aspects of Learning (SEAL) programme is now being rolled out nationally in primary schools.

Each local authority in England will have at least one behaviour and attendance consultant who will work closely with schools giving advice, delivering training, supporting the audit process and linking with behaviour support services. Access to this support will normally be through the local authority inclusion/pupil support section or through the behaviour support services. As the consultants cover a large number of schools, they will have knowledge of successful practices locally and be able to 'buddy up' schools to support and/or share good practices. Staff visiting other schools is an invaluable way of getting ideas and sharing resources.

The DfES *Pupil Support Circular 10/99* gave some very good practical guidance in working with pupils with behaviour difficulties. Recently some parts of this guidance have been updated, and have provide some useful tips and ideas that can be shared with staff and used to challenge thinking in schools.

The *Exclusions Guidance Part 1: Promoting Positive Behaviour and Early Intervention* (DfES, 2004) gives a helpful checklist of ideas for working with pupils who have behaviour difficulties. Key points/ideas arising are:

- The importance of behaviour policies, procedures and training – this needs to be done on a whole-school and department basis, permeating all aspects of school life and, in particular, teaching and learning in the classroom.

- The need for a range of measures and flexible use of resources such as engaging parents, changing classes/groups and developing a package of curriculum alternatives at any Key Stage but particularly a Key Stage 4, age range in Scotland, 14–16-year-olds. This could include college, work, training or other forms of alternative provision.

- A temporary placement in a learning support unit (LSU) – as part of a planned programme. This is expanded further in this chapter, however, it is essential to point out that LSUs must not be seen as a 'sin bin', otherwise the pupil may never see the light of day again. Also the LSU manager must be able to get out and work in the classroom, otherwise the school will have a disaffected LSU manager on its hands as well as pupils.

- Temporary or part-time placement in a pupil referral unit (PRU). In theory this is available, but PRUs are rapidly filling up with pupils who stay a long time, and therefore PRUs have little flexibility to respond to shorter placements or support work in schools. This, in turn, has a knock-on effect for some LSUs that are full of pupils who will not move back into class or other provision outside the school. As a result of this, some schools have developed a range of provision to meet longer-term needs of pupils, for example, separate classes within the school.

- A managed move to another school. This procedure is part of an overall policy developed by the headteachers of schools in the local area. A protocol is agreed and the move for the pupil is a planned and supported one, rather than a 'get out quick' response or a suggestion to parents that their child would be better off in another school so as to avoid the exclusion figures increasing. Many managed-move protocols involve support from the behaviour support services, educational welfare and other appropriate agencies. A plan is drawn up to support the pupil's move to another school which is agreed by the pupil, family, receiving school and referring school. In reality the plan should consist of a gradual introduction to the receiving school with all staff aware of the pupil and his or her needs, the LSU often being involved as a halfway house. The move is then managed by identified professionals who will then monitor progress until the pupil is fully settled. It is in the interests of all schools for this to take place, otherwise pupils move from school to school and no one benefits. In the Scunthorpe area this was known as the 'Scunthorpe shuffle'. On the CD, Chapter 2 Example 1 is a managed move protocol devised by Enfield between schools and Enfield local authority.

- Assessment of special educational needs including a possible placement in a Special School. In reality, this is a difficult option for pupils at the latter end of Key Stages 3 and 4, age range 12–16 year-olds-in Scotland, owing to the time it takes to statement and the fact that many SEBD Special Schools are full. The earlier a statement is pursued, say in primary school or at the beginning of Key Stage 3, the better the chance of a positive outcome. Many pupils with complex behaviour difficulties will have exhibited difficulties in the early years. Therefore, resources should be made available through Children's Services at that stage to meet the needs of the pupil, family, carers and school. However, many Special Schools are now developing outreach support which could be of benefit to both the pupil and the mainstream school.

- Allocation of a key worker such as a learning mentor, Connexions personal adviser, education welfare officer (EWO) and so on. This is good advice: schools need to have effective co-ordination and to share information on a systematic basis. The lead professional role is discussed in Chapter 4. It is important that the pupil has an identified person whom they can relate to.

- Referral to a specialist support service such as the Child and Adolescence Mental Health Services (CAMHS), educational welfare and so on. Access to these services is becoming more effective through local partnership working and the Behaviour and Education Support Teams; however, access to mental health services still remains problematic in many areas. Schools are therefore appointing their own staff to undertake these duties, including therapists and counsellors. Just being told by a consultant psychiatrist that a pupil has a conduct disorder does not help in their management. Schools need practical help and strategies that are seen through.

- Pastoral Support Plans (PSPs) – these are useful in setting out the range of strategies/ support that needs to be in place during a set period of time. Guidance on these should be available from the Education Department or Children's Services Team. Leeds Behaviour and Attendance Service has produced some effective examples and guidance around PSPs (www.educationleeds.co.uk).

The guidance also outlines a number of other good practice examples:

- Restorative justice, which brings the 'offender' and the 'victim' together to resolve the situation.

- Mediation through a third party – LSU staff have been successful in these areas, particularly between pupil and teacher, when the pupil needs to go back into a mainstream class. A meeting is held with the pupil, the teacher and the LSU or learning mentor to discuss the difficulties and plan strategies to take the situation forward.

- Internal seclusion (we now have inclusion, exclusion and seclusion), which is a time-out provision, not an LSU, but a short, time-limited removal from class into a well-ordered environment within the school. Internal seclusion should be seen as part of a continuum of support for pupils with behaviour difficulties and should be used within clear and consistent criteria. Monitoring of pupils and staff who use this facility will give an indication not only of pupil difficulties, but also subject and individual teacher issues. This data can then be passed on to department/subject co-ordinators.

Part 7 of the *Exclusions Guidance: LEA Responsibility to Provide Full-Time Education and Re-integrate Permanently Excluded Pupils* (DfES, 2004) is a useful document for schools as it outlines the role of the local education authority (LEA), pupil referral units and other provision for permanently excluded pupils. The DfES will publish guidance on the role of remove rooms and the inspection of LSUs in 2006. There is helpful information on reintegration, planning, panels, steps towards successful placements, transition issues and work with colleges of further education (FE).

Suggestions for making it happen ...

- Schools need to have time to plan, research and audit current practice in order to start to write behaviour policies. Involve governors where possible.

- Audit the different types of behaviours that pupils present. A behaviour database could be used, such as Sleuth www.schoolsoftwarecompany.com or a customised database from the behaviour support services in your local area. These databases will give information on frequency and types of behaviour which will allow schools to plan and deploy their resources.

- Identify the range of support service provision that is available including Special Schools – establish a database of contacts.

- Ensure there is consistent use and understanding of the terminology related to pupil behaviour.

- Make contact with the behaviour and attendance consultant in your particular local authority area. They mostly deal with Key Stages 3 and 4, but also do some work at

> primary level with behaviour support services and PRUs that cater for Key Stage 2. They are a useful source of advice and support.
>
> ■ Check to see whether there is a managed move protocol in place in the local area.
>
> ■ Establish a budget for the range of support with the senior leadership team.
>
> ■ Check out referral procedures and systems of the various agencies/services. Use this information to shape the provision in school and to ensure that the various systems complement, not duplicate, each other.

Accessing support from other agencies

In many cases schools are thwarted in their attempts to engage outside agency services because of the procedures that many have to go through to obtain a referral. While it is appreciated that schools will have different thresholds/tolerance and skills in working with pupils who have a range of barriers to learning, it is important for specialist services to realise that many schools are developing substantial capacity to meet these pupils' needs and want a fast and appropriate response when a difficult problem occurs.

There is an opportunity within the Children's Services developments to approach referral in a completely different way and encourage more professional debate and sharing of ideas. It is recognised by many who work in schools that there are key milestones in a pupil's life where changes/developments happen and can be spotted. To break this referral 'log jam', agencies and schools can look upon these milestones as an opportunity to enter into professional debate, sharing practice, ideas and information to help schools and others make more effective provision all round and make best use of the professional expertise. This concept would allow schools and others to break away from a total referral culture, where little professional debate is had with schools and everything is about filling in forms.

Suggested milestones could be the following ages:

■ 3 years – early trigger signs picked up by the early intervention team who support the family as well as the child.

■ 5 years – much of the Sure Start, early years intervention and parenting support ceases and schools take on much of that responsibility.

■ 7 years – recognised as a stage where pupils show learning and behavioural difficulties which appear in accessing the curriculum.

■ 9 years – two years before transfer to secondary, challenges of the curriculum in evidence, enough time to put in place some effective strategies before moving onto secondary school.

■ 13 years – before options and preparation for transition planning, signs of disengagement appearing.

■ 16 years– transition to the next steps for the future.

This process would be helpful for those pupils with a wide range of barriers to learning. More complex needs could have the additional multi-agency support that comes with a statement or with access to a child development centre for the early/primary years. A suggested way forward for schools would be to:

- undertake an analysis of the pupils in your school who might benefit from this approach; collate the data showing types of need and the kind of discussion/input that would be useful

- contact inclusion colleagues in neighbouring schools to see if they would be interested, because the more schools who want to undertake this the more chance that there is of services responding; a pilot area could be chosen

- contact the local authority inclusion manager to share ideas and assess the possibility of systemising meetings with specific agencies around the milestone times: it maybe helpful to choose two or three key agencies such as educational psychologists, therapists and social services, and much will depend on the phase of working, with early years support being key in the early years and personal advisers being important in Key Stages 3 and 4

- suggest a trial period with an evaluation of the process. This can then be shared with others to inform future practice.

Suggestions for making it happen ...

- Ensure that there is a multi-agency strategy in place in order to implement professional debate at each milestone.

- Agencies need to develop a greater understanding of the capacity and confidence of schools in dealing with pupils with SEBD in order that the response to need can be appropriate, flexible and not over-bureaucratic.

- Share best practice around working with families in order to continue effective working practices across the life of the pupil in and before school, in college and beyond.

- Audit the skills offered and the training needs of school staff; audit the skills and training opportunities offered by the multidisciplinary teams and match the two in order to produce a processional development training plan, some of which can be met in house, but other support will need to be purchased from outside.

- Appoint an overall co-ordinator for this range of services who can have open and transparent dialogue with schools.

- Produce a booklet outlining the range of services for parents and schools on support, access to provision and so on for pupils with SEBD.

- Establish a forum, in conjunction with other schools and the local authority, across the services, to discuss, advise and implement policy and strategy with regard to pupils with SEBD.

Specific Programmes

Inclusion in the early years

The government has focused on early support through the Early Support Pilot Programme (ESPP). Early support is now a key government priority and it is seeking to improve services nationally, regionally and locally for disabled children and their families. Early Support involves the DfES, Sure Start and the Department of Health. It supports families and people working for education, health, social services and the voluntary sector. Many local authorities now offer an integrated approach to early years and childcare services via Early Years Development and Childcare Partnerships.

The recent OFSTED report, *Removing Barriers: A 'Can-do' Attitude: A Report on Developing Good Practice for Children with Special Needs in Early Years Childcare and Education in the Private and Voluntary Sectors,* is a useful reference. It examines how childcare providers are making it easier for children with special needs to access care and education and have the best possible outcomes. Key factors for good practice include:

- having a 'can-do' attitude

- effective partnerships with parents

- joined up support from other agencies

- good leadership

- access to training.

There are a number of programmes catering specifically for very young children which schools will find useful.

Sure Start

Sure Start children's centres in England provide early education integrated with health and family support services along with childcare from 8 a.m. to 6 p.m. Services are open to parents with babies and young children together with their grandparents, childminders and other carers. Sure Start centres provide a wide range of services including drop-in centres, parent and toddler groups, specialist advice on issues such as health, housing and benefits, training programmes including parenting courses, and social events. Some schools have Sure Start centres on their premises while others can access the support in local community settings. Schools will find this service helpful in:

- supporting vulnerable families

- offering training and up-to-date information for school staff

- supporting the transition of pupils into school

- ensuring that communication and information are shared effectively and that there is continuity and consistency of support where appropriate.

Children's centres are models of integrated service provision and contribute directly to the *Every Child Matters* outcomes. Many will be based in primary schools. This will enable those schools to be at the heart of the local community's multidisciplinary approach. The advantages for schools in having a centre as part of their provision is great. In particular those of:

■ ready access to support services

■ providing a continuum and consistency of provision for the pupil and family from early years to secondary school

■ a co-ordinated approach to the family and early identification of need.

The Portage service

The service provides a regular (usually weekly) home visit by a trained home visitor, who works in partnership with the parent(s) to promote their child's development. This involves using play and a range of toys and equipment to stimulate the child's involvement and to work on any areas of concern regarding their development, for example, language or behaviour. Schools will find the service useful in:

■ accessing information, by agreement with all parties, that will help plan for the pupil's smooth entry into school

■ providing additional support and advice for staff in meeting the needs of the pupil

■ sharing resources and strategies to improve the capacity of the school to respond to need.

There is an extensive Portage network across the UK, overseen by the National Portage Association, see website www.portage.org.uk.

Nurture groups

Nurture groups have been in existence since the 1970s in primary and infant schools although they are growing in popularity in secondary schools. In essence, they are small classes for pupils with an identified need, often those with social, emotional or behavioural difficulties. The group usually has a teacher and an assistant. Pupils attend the group on a sessional or part-time basis, following an adapted curriculum matched to their needs. The curriculum places an emphasis on communication, language and interaction with peers. The work is intensive and there is close liaison between the nurture group teacher and assistant, the class teacher and parents over the precise programme. Schools which have nurture groups have praised their impact on pupils' social, communication and emotional well-being. In some areas local education authorities have part funded the groups while others have obtained funding through EiC or other similar funding routes. There is a nurture group network with a website (www.nurturegroups.org), and they will be happy to send examples of good practice and give practical advice on establishing the programme in your school.

Moving onto other programmes that can straddle the phases.

Learning support units

Learning support units have been a strand of the Excellence in Cities programme since 1999, although many schools have had similar provision for some time before that date. In essence they are resource centres designed to meet the needs of pupils who:

- have poor anger management skills

- find it difficult to accept sanctions

- show a lack of respect for authority

- are aggressive, insolent and belligerent

- have poor social and communication skills

- are shy, withdrawn and anxious

- are long-term absentees

- are victims of bullying, robberies or domestic violence

- find adjusting to new situations difficult – that is, pupils in transition, those who cannot cope with large institutions, and asylum seekers and refugees.

Each unit or centre will be slightly different in each school depending on the context of the school and the range of needs that the pupils present. Many are not called units and instead use a variety of names that reflect the kind of provision the school wishes to evolve.

Learning support units should:

- be an integral part of the school approach to learning and behaviour support

- provide separate short-term teaching and support programmes tailored to the needs of pupils

- provide sectional support to work with pupils at an early stage

- facilitate the reintegration of pupils into mainstream classes

- devise and support individual curriculum and behaviour packages.

They are not:

- long-term respite care

- a 'sin bin' or dumping ground

- a facility for extremely challenging pupils who should be in a specialised environment

- an isolated bolt-on provision (*Good Practice Guidelines for Learning Support Units* – DfES, 2002).

In essence LSUs are an integral part of the continuum of pupils who have specific needs and barriers to learning. They are not a remove room, seclusion, exclusion or time-out room. The

LSU should provide targeted support within the whole-school Behaviour and Inclusion Policy and Strategy.

Learning support units are now established in both primary and secondary schools. There is clear evidence from OFSTED inspection reports that they have had a significant impact on reducing exclusion, and improving the attendance and attainment of many pupils, and have improved pupils' self-image and self-worth, which has enabled them to have a more positive outlook on life. Some of the best practice is in Key Stage 1 where a real multi-professional approach can be established as well as strong links with families and carers. Learning support units that cater for mainly Key Stage 4 pupils tend not to reintegrate many pupils into mainstream classes (as in most cases it is too late) but concentrate on a flexible curriculum package that consists of work placement, key skills, college and training provider placement/courses. Transition into work or further education must be a driving force for many pupils at this stage.

In planning an LSU, schools need to ensure that there is:

- time set aside for planning, finding out about practice elsewhere and reading the DfES good practice guidelines on LSUs; there are regional support officers who advise on good practice within LSUs and can support and train staff (further details can be obtained from the Dfes website www.dfes.gov.uk/sie/eic/lsu).

- a clear remit, entry and exit criteria that is fully understood by all staff

- trained and qualified staff to run the centre who have flexibility to work alongside classroom teachers to help and improve practice

- an appropriate location for the base which is at the heart of the school and also used by multidisciplinary professionals.

Maltby Comprehensive School in Rotherham has listed the factors that have contributed to the success of their LSU and can be found on the CD, Chapter 2, Example 2, and will be useful for schools to consider when planning their provision.

Learning mentors

Learning mentors were first introduced as part of the Excellence in Cities programme in 1999. The concept was of creating a professional who was not a teacher but who was available to listen, talk things through and help plan support with pupils who have a range of barriers to learning. This role has proved to be one of the most successful and innovative programmes in schools over the past 20 years. A learning mentor acts as a:

- role model

- listener and observer

- supporter and encourager

- professional friend

- challenger of assumptions

- guide

- target negotiator.

A Learning mentor is *not* a:

- counsellor – unless they have a diploma in counselling

- classroom assistant

- babysitter

- corridor monitor

- disciplinarian

- person to whom a child is sent when naughty. (*Good Practice Guidelines for Learning Mentors* – DfES, 2002)

The prime aim of the role is to improve pupils' attainment, motivation, behaviour, attendance and attitude to learning. Further aims are to reduce exclusions as well as to work towards removing particular barriers to learning, including the mental health issues that a wide number of pupils present.

Learning mentors work within the context of the school, and the identified range of needs may vary from school to school. Specific roles are now emerging to meet specific needs, such as a learning mentor for transition, behaviour, study support, reintegration and so on.

The impact of the role has been immense and is frequently recognised in OFSTED and Her Majesty's Inspectorate (HMI) inspections reports. The key impact has been

on individual pupils:

- providing a support network

- raising attainment and achievement while reducing exclusion

- improvement of social skills, self-esteem, confidence and motivation

- improved relationship with peers, families and staff

- improved organisational skills

- pupils own the problem and resolve difficulties

- supporting parents and carers/pupils in resolving and handling conflicts in a positive way;

on school standards:

- increase in attainment

- improved communication with teachers, managers, governors and agencies about the progress of individual pupils

- increase in extra-curricular activities and additional qualifications

- expertise of learning mentors used to develop a range of activities and curriculum developments across the school

- improved image of pupil support across the school – it is cool to have a mentor

- earlier intervention as learning mentors are around and available at different points during the day to work with pupils' behaviour problems

- learning mentors play a key role in delivering the five outcomes of *Every Child Matters* and the government agenda for personalised learning.

The range of support that learning mentors provide can be endless – examples include specific group work on anger management, circle time, self-esteem/confidence/assertiveness courses, lunchtime and after-school activities, drop-in clubs, breakfast clubs, specific curriculum support groups and individual one-to-one work through an identified caseload system. Much work has been achieved working with families and carers, managing the transition between schools and mid-term entry problems, and in co-ordinating services and supporting programmes with a range of multidisciplinary professionals. One successful lunchtime club in a secondary school was called the 'Get on Club' for those pupils who did not get on. Another was called 'A Step in Confidence' course, which is a programme for those pupils who find working in groups difficult and need some space to develop their self-esteem and practical strategies to use in unfamiliar settings.

Part of the success of the programme is that learning mentors come with different backgrounds, skills and experience. Many live within the school's local community and reflect the ethnic mix of the school population. Young male black learning mentors have been highly successful in identifying and working with young black and Asian boys to act as a role model. Many learning mentors can speak other languages and these have been used to build a bridge between the school and those families where English is little spoken or understood.

As with other members of the Inclusion Team, learning mentors require a base with access to a telephone and computer, and an area for both group and confidential individual work. Training and induction is important for this role, further information on this is in Chapter 3. The learning mentor co-ordinators have been key to the success of the role in providing support, guidance and training packages to suit learning mentors' needs.

In establishing learning mentor provision schools should:

- identify the groups/cohorts of pupils that require support

- investigate other practice using the *DfES Good Practice Guidelines for Learning Mentors* (DfES, 2002) and the recently published *Supporting the New Agenda for Children's Services and School: The Role of Learning Mentors and Co-ordinators* (DfES, 2005); Visit the learning mentor website www.standards.dfes.gov.uk/learningmentors which has a range of downloadable resources; also contact the local learning mentor co-ordinator in the local authority who will offer advice and support

- ensure that the role is clearly understood by all staff and that clear management of the role is in place. An example of a learning mentor action plan and deployment is on the CD, Chapter 2 Example 3.

Learning mentors play a key role in delivering the five outcomes of *Every Child Matters* and the government agenda for personalised learning.

Behaviour Improvement Programme

The Behaviour Improvement Programme (BIP) is a key part of the national Behaviour and Attendance Strategy. It is targeted alongside the Excellence in Cities programme and those identified schools in the EiC areas. This programme, along with EiC will still be operating in some form after April 2006 but the funding methodology will change. The ideas and strategies do form the basis of good practice Much advice and many ideas can be gained from the programme even if your school is not part of the designated area for support.

The key objectives of the BIP are around the provision of full-time provision for excluded pupils, an audited and structured approach to managing behaviour in schools, reduction of truancy and the appointment of additional staff, particularly those from multidisciplinary backgrounds, to work in innovative ways to support vulnerable pupils and their families.

Each area will have developed a range of provision depending on the context and the needs of the schools where poor attendance and truancy are significant barriers to learning. The programme supports strategies already in place and provides the resources to develop additional measures to support schools. Schools have used the BIP resources in a variety of ways to establish better systems and means of intervening earlier to support pupils at risk of exclusion.

The most effective practices have shown the following characteristics:

- focusing on prevention because of the potential offered by the additional resources

- commitment from schools to reducing exclusion

- measures based on the analysis of quantitative and qualitative data to determine the main drivers behind misbehaviour leading to exclusion

- installation of systems for tracking behaviour across the school day, enabling the School Leadership Team to identify the pressure points and places

- placing a high priority on preventative strategies backed with sufficient resources to enable full implementation and sustainability

- providing contingency resources for cases where exclusion is the appropriate response to pupil misbehaviour

- proactively seeking and co-ordinating resources to support prevention, including close liaison with Behaviour Support Services and Education Welfare Services

- linking the BIP strategy and associated funding to the 14–19 age-group strategies in terms of providing alternative curricular opportunities and approaches.

A number of schools have adopted a collaborative approach to working with pupils with behaviour difficulties. The key elements of good practice have included:

- shared agreement between schools on whole-school behaviour policies and practices

- shared and agreed protocols on procedures and staffing – including transporting the pupils to another school

- regular meetings of headteachers to discuss the causes of exclusions

- a leadership role for the local authority in holding the group together and tackling potential barriers to progress

- an effective information-sharing system between schools so that they are aware at all times of a pupil's whereabouts and learning activity.

A number of schools have developed formal seclusion policies. Seclusion units or on-site exclusion centres can be used as part of a preventative strategy. This model is particularly helpful to overcome some of the difficult issues associated with re integration following exclusion. Systematic planning is needed to ensure that there are clear procedures about the use of this measure and that these are communicated to staff, governors, pupils and parents. Schools wishing to implement any of these strategies need to:

- visit the website of the behaviour and attendance programme www.dfes.gov.uk/behaviourandattendance/, which gives a range of contacts, resources and good practice examples

- decide through an audit of need in the school the key priority areas and whether the ideas generated through the BIP programme can be of use

- plan the intervention within the inclusion strategy and have a key manager responsible for the implementation.

As part of the BIP programme multi-agency teams were established called Behaviour Education and Support Teams. These teams brought together a complementary mix of professionals from the field of health, social care and education. The aim of a BEST is to promote emotional well-being, positive behaviour and school attendance by identifying and supporting those with, or at risk of developing, emotional and behavioural problems. They work with children and young people aged 5–18, their families and schools to intervene early and prevent problems developing further. Many are placed at the heart of a community of primary and secondary schools. A typical team may include the following:

- psychologists – clinical/educational

- health visitors

- school nurses

- mental health workers

- behaviour support staff

- education welfare staff

- social/family workers

- range of therapists.

These teams have been invaluable in supporting pupils and their families as well as schools in terms of quick routes to referral and additional professional expertise when working with staff and training on a whole-school basis.

Skill Force

The Skill Force programme was originally conceived by the Ministry of Defence to enable pupils in Key Stage 4 to experience a range of curricular and extra-curricular activities provided by officers of the forces. In April 2004, Skill Force became an independent organisation with teams of ex-forces officers around the country delivering a range of courses such as Duke of Edinburgh Award, ASDAN and a variety of sporting awards in secondary schools. This programme has had a significant effect on improving pupils' behaviour, attendance and motivation. Skill force has become a key part of the Behaviour Improvement Programme across the UK. (See website www.skillforce.org)

Attendance and punctuality

Alongside the Behaviour Strategy is the Attendance Strategy, which is key to improving pupil attainment and attendance and reducing exclusion. It is an important element in any inclusion policy because if pupils are not at school, they are not going to learn and could be at risk of anti-social behaviour and criminal activities. Non-attendance could also be linked to the range of barriers to learning presented throughout the chapters of this book.

Each local authority will have a behaviour and attendance consultant; many will have a range of support in addition to this role, such as attendance officers and educational welfare officers. Many schools, as a result of programmes and initiatives, have started to appoint their own attendance team or create a specific attendance role within a cluster of schools that is responsible to the schools and not to the local authority. Initiatives using electronic registration systems have been useful in order to synchronise attendance procedures and highlight problems at an early stage. These have been particularly useful in secondary schools to track attendance throughout the day and spot patterns and issues. In one school there was very poor attendance and lateness on certain days: when investigated, there was a high correlation with assemblies.

New strategies have been piloted around fast-tracking to court parents who condone the absence of their children. New guidance came into force in September 2005, on penalty notices, parenting contracts and parenting orders. Local authorities, school governing bodies, school staff and the police, including community support officers, are required by law to have regard to this guidance. This means that, although the guidance does not have the force of statute, there is an expectation that the guidance will be followed unless there is a good reason to depart from it. Judgement will need to take account of the circumstances of individual cases.

There is a wealth of invaluable information on the Tackling it Together – Working Together to Raise Attendance website (www.dfes.gov.uk/schoolattendance/goodpractice/tackling.cfm) with good practice publications on:

- attendance policy and projects
- fast-track attendance cases
- holidays in term time, and study leave

- multi-agency initiatives

- parenting contracts and notices

- Service Level Agreements.

Punctuality also has a real impact on attainment, attendance and exclusion. It is probably a more frustrating and difficult problem than attendance itself. In one primary school there were concerns over the attainment of a group of girls at Key Stage 2. When investigated further, it turned out that they were young carers and were often late because of having to take siblings to the doctors or other schools, doing shopping and so on, and this had a direct impact on their performance at school. Once recognised, the learning mentor could target time and support at alleviating the situation and working with the families and other agencies to support the girls. Quite often, learning mentors wait outside the school at the beginning of the day for parents who bring their children in late. They then work with the family to look at ideas on how to manage a family setting off to different places at the same time.

Lateness into lessons causes many behaviour difficulties to emerge. Sometimes schools can be seen as just social centres, as pupils gather around the corridors having been sent out of lesson and no one being available to pick them up or challenge them. The 'late book' holds the key to many issues of attendance and behaviour in schools. Often it is taken by an administrative assistant who, in the eyes of the pupil, has little 'clout' in terms of challenge as to the reason for lateness. If this is allowed to continue and is not overseen by a senior member of staff then mayhem will rule. In one school there were over 100 late arrivals in one day but no one was challenging the pupils or looking at the pattern of punctuality and linking this to behaviour issues. As soon as this was realised and dealt with effectively, behaviour started to improve. There has to be a clear cut-off point when the 'late book' is shut and absence begins.

Although an old cliché, the approach has to involve the whole school and staff must take responsibility for starting and finishing lessons on time, and for tackling pupils who are in corridors and the playground after lessons have started. School routines are very important and the movement of pupils around the school has a direct impact on the punctuality and attitude of pupils to their work.

The following is an example of an attendance aide-memoire and it is a useful checklist for schools when auditing the school's provision for promoting good attendance and punctuality. The completion of this document would aid the school in looking at gaps and celebrating areas of good practice.

Many schools are now using educational welfare officers in a variety of ways such as supporting attendance audits, working with groups of pupils and their families and delivering aspects of the PHSE curriculum. They need to be part of the Inclusion Team and to work flexibly across the school. Some schools have appointed their own welfare officers or share them between clusters of schools.

Attendance Aide-Memoire

Suggested questions/areas for discussion

Management issues

- Does improving attendance/punctuality have any priority in the school development plan? Are there target figures for attendance/punctuality?

- Is there any budget attached to securing improvement such as the use of inclusion monies, pupil retention grants?

- Is there any hard evidence that the school has analysed the impact that poor attendance is having on standards?

- Was attendance/punctuality an issue in the previous OFSTED report? If so, what action has been taken and has there been any improvement?

- Does the school use manual or OMR registration recording? If so is the information broken down by year groups/cohorts/ethnicity/SEN/looked after pupils/refugee/asylum seekers and so on?

- Is there any correlation between attendance patterns, attainment and standards and behavioural incidents in the school?

- Is there a weekly production of a summary of attendance that is acted upon?

- Who in the school has the responsibility for monitoring attendance? What action is taken and how soon?

- Is there any analysis of lesson registers to pick out if particular lessons are not being attended?

- Does whoever monitors the registers have a good knowledge of child protection procedures? Are there secure links with social services' area child protection committee to alert appropriate services when there is a pattern of absence or lack of punctuality that gives concern?

- What liaison is there with the education welfare service and other agencies?

- What work has been done with parents regarding non-attendance? Are there formal interviews with parents/pupils about punctuality/attendance?

- What is the role and success of the learning mentors with attendance issues?

Systems and procedures

- Are codes for absence used in registers? Do they clearly distinguish between absences and do not for example employ a generic code, a catch all, that gives no clear picture of why pupils are away?

- When are registers closed?

- Are absence codes consistent across the school and authority?

- Is there a firm procedure for sending pro forma letters, signed by senior members of staff at determined intervals, to obtain reasons for absences/recurring lateness, prior to marking the absence unauthorised?

- What reasons do non-attenders give when asked why they do not bother coming to school?

- Are there absence report forms completed by form tutors/class teachers where there are concerns?

- Are messages to the school about absences, for example, from parents, recorded in a message book, with dates and times of messages?

- Does the school ensure that telephoning home on the first day of absence takes place and, if so, how early in the morning is it done?

- Are all registers completed at each registration, for example, does each pupil have a mark against their name whether they are in class or not?

- Is there a 'late book' or a 'signing in/out book' for pupils in order that they can be tracked in and out of the building? Is there weekly monitoring of a 'late book'?

- Do pupils have a pass/authorisation when they leave the classroom?

- Are there any 'in-school' sanctions for being late, for example, detentions?

In-school implementation

- Are previous weeks' attendance figures displayed for pupils?

- Are target figures for attendance highlighted on classroom/form room doors?

- Does the school use full attendance as part of a reward system for individuals and groups?

- Do pupils have any responsibility to complete their own attendance profile; for example, showing their targets?

- Are there any attendance graphs around school? Any attendance trophies? Do any local businesses sponsor rewards for good attendance?

- Is there any emphasis in secondary schools in encouraging attendance or rewarding attendance in year 7?

- Are there any programmes in year 6 to highlight the importance of attendance on transfer to secondary school?

- Are any CCTV cameras installed? Is there any co-ordination of CCTV cameras with, for example, an entry phone to the school?

- Has the school considered/actioned a change in curriculum especially for Key Stage 4 pupils to encourage better attendance, punctuality and retention?

- Have you any success stories which you would like to share?

Future provision and support

- What kind of support/guidance would you like from the local authority and other support services in order to improve attendance and punctuality in school?

Connexions service

The impact of Connexions personal advisers has varied across the country, and the government now sees a change of role, with schools taking much more ownership of the process. Responsibility for commissioning information, advice and guidance (IAG) and funding that goes with it will move from the Connexions service to local authorities, working through Children's Trusts, schools and colleges. High performing Connexions services will be preserved and, in most cases, Children's Trusts, schools and colleges will agree on new arrangements for commissioning IAG locally. However, where local provision is poor, schools and colleges will have the right to commission the service directly from other providers. The new arrangements are expected to be in place by 2008. Personal advisers have been most successful when they have had significant time in a school, thereby developing programmes and relationships which are sustainable. They can be a very effective member of the Inclusion Team, focusing on the hardest to reach pupils in Key Stage 4 and linking with colleges, work training providers and co-ordinating the various agencies. Many work closely with learning mentors on individual pupils and in running specific sessions on motivation, organisational skills and anger management.

Special Schools Specialist Status Programme

The government is keen that Special Schools are recognised for the excellent practice that is currently in place and that they share and develop their practice. In December 2005, the DfES launched the Special Schools Specialist Status Programme, based on the four areas of the *SEN Code of Practice* in terms of areas of need:

- cognition and learning

- behaviour and emotional

- communication and interaction

- sensory and physical.

The Specialist Status Programme is part of the wider mainstream school specialist programme. Special Schools who gain this status will have a particular strength not only in their specified area but in outreach support and community partnerships. Mainstream schools will benefit greatly from this expertise. There is also a specialist SEN status now being awarded to mainstream schools; details of both these programmes can be obtained from www.standards.dfes.gov.uk/specialistschools.

Selecting and co-ordinating programmes

Clearly, it is important to choose the most appropriate programme(s) for your particular school's circumstances. If you are using a range of initiatives, it is essential that these are co-ordinated and that there is joined-up thinking, planning and management as part of a coherent programme. Many of the initiatives described can make a valuable contribution to the *Every Child Matters* agenda. Any initiatives selected need to be clearly linked with the five key outcomes of *Every Child Matters* and their impact monitored and regularly reviewed. Effective communication among all those involved is also essential.

Funding

The specific programmes described in this chapter have mainly been resourced through additional funding from EiC and the BIP. While this funding has been confined to schools in qualifying areas, many other schools across the UK have taken on and shared practice. For those schools who have received additional funding, this will remain after the national changes to funding in 2006. However, local partnerships of headteachers can choose to reallocate funds and realign budgets if there have been little outcomes from existing programmes. From 2006, all schools will be funded in a different way with an overall delegated budget, which will give greater flexibility for schools to work with pupils in a variety of different ways and much more opportunity to integrate initiatives effectively.

All schools can learn from these programmes, whether they have been a part of the initiatives or not; the challenge is to share information and best practice so that provision for pupils improves across the board.

Suggestions for making it happen ...

- Ensure that you have undertaken a thorough audit of pupils' needs in the school.

- Analyse existing practice as to what works well and what needs to be changed.

- In light of the above, select the most appropriate range of programmes and initiatives that meet the specific needs of the pupils and the context of the school.

- Ensure that programmes and initiatives fit the *Every Child Matters* agenda.

- Take key members of staff with you – all staff need to be involved in this process. It is also important that staff skills are known and utilised to best effect.

- The Inclusion Team needs to work with classroom teachers, subject departments and faculties to integrate inclusion best practice into their work.

- Make opportunities to work in classes and track specific groups of pupils to see where the pressure points are.

- Use a range of staff, teaching assistants, learning mentors and so on to look at lunchtime hot spots and practical solutions that can be put in place. Examples include playground games, use of equipment, Breakfast Clubs, lunchtime activities, homework clubs, the Get on Club at one high school for those pupils who could not get on.

- Research different funding routes and how these can be used most effectively – schools may wish to do this as a joint venture.

Look it up ...

■ Early Years programmes, www.everychildmatters.gov.uk

■ Tackling It Together – Working Together to Raise Attendance www.dfes.gov.uk/sch oolattendance/goodpractice/tackling.cfm

■ Connexions, www.connexions.gov.uk

■ Special Schools Specialist Programme, www.standards.dfes.gov.uk/specialistschools

■ Extended Services in School – Baseline Summary of Maintained Schools in 2005, www.teachernet.gov.uk

CHAPTER 3

Developing an Inclusive School

In this chapter we look at how to work towards an inclusive school and how to get it right. If you are going to create a successful inclusive school, it is essential that you plan the inclusion programme carefully. Creating an inclusion strategy is the key to this. The strategy will bring together all the elements of inclusion in one succinct document and will form the basis for the school's inclusion policy. It also forms an important part of the self-evaluation and monitoring process. This chapter also looks at inclusion policies, inclusion structures and models, and the importance of effective inclusion training.

Developing an inclusion strategy

All too often, strategies are bible-sized documents which sit on a shelf gathering dust and are only produced when the OFSTED inspector visits. If you are serious about creating a truly inclusive school, you need to develop a strategy which is succinct (no more than 15 sides of A4 paper) and in plain English, is developed by a representative group of people from within and outside the school, and has the backing of all those involved in inclusion in the school. This is no mean feat but, with careful planning and management, will make the difference between success and failure. It is also important to be aware that the government has now established three-year budgets, which means that those involved in managing and implementing the inclusion agenda within schools and other agencies will enjoy a greater level of stability and be able to develop longer-term strategic planning, particularly around staffing.

Strategy framework and contents

The following is a suggested framework and contents for an inclusion strategy – clearly, there will be specific issues within each school, however, the following headings are universal and form a useful starting point for structuring your strategy effectively.

Executive summary/foreword

- A short (one side) summary of the strategy.

Introduction

- Why the strategy is being developed.

  - National and local context:

  - overview of the current national legislation and requirements as set out in Chapter 1

  - overview of the local context within which the school is operating, that is, socio-economic and demographic make-up of school pupils; specific pupil needs; current initiatives; attainment levels; funding arrangements and so on, in other words, where are we now?

- SWOT (strengths/weaknesses/opportunities/threats) analysis of current provision.

- Links with other strategies/plans/policies – to ensure that they are all complementary.

Overall purpose of strategy

To establish an inclusion policy for (a.n. other) school which meets the needs of pupils and parents, sets clear guidance for staff and other agencies, and ensures the school meets its legal requirements in relation to SEN guidance, *Every Child Matters* and the Children's Services framework.

Strategy partnership and consultation

- Who is involved in developing the strategy? It is important to involve pupils, staff, parents and other agencies.

- Who are the consultees for the strategy? How and when will consultation be undertaken?

Key issues

For each of the following key issues, there needs to be a broad set of key actions with performance measures and targets as appropriate.

1. Strategic planning and leadership

- Key roles of governors, senior managers and inclusion manager.

- Decision-making processes.

- Role of local authority.

- Advisory groups and working parties.

- Links with schools and other agencies within and outside the area.

- Use of common terminology.

2. Identification and intervention

- Baseline assessments.

- Use of prior information.

- Pupil induction procedures.

- Information flow – confidentiality issues.

- Identification strategies – range of measures.

- Early intervention – inclusion panels; support prior to significant action.

- School action strategies.

- Role of subject/class teacher in identification.

- Tracking methodology – who teaches pupils? Are they making sufficient progress?

- Referral procedures.

- Whole-school databases.

- Common Assessment Framework.

3. Access and support

In the context of inclusive learning, access needs to be seen in terms of physical access, access to the curriculum and access to information.

- Physical access:

    - Physical access is largely driven by DDA legislation. It is important to note that the legislation also goes beyond physical access and looks at issues such as ethos, culture and support.

    - The DDA audit needs to cover physical issues, transport arrangements, access to equipment and resources along with the other issues of ethos, quality of support and culture. The audit should result in recommendations which ensure that physical access meets the needs of the pupils and makes maximum use of resources to ensure best value. (See CD, Chapter 3 Example 1 for helpful suggestions to make this happen.)

- Access to the curriculum:

    - Specialist learning resources required to meet needs.

    - Database of resources – within and outside different agencies; Special School resources.

    - Use of ICT – software/hardware.

    - Differentiation strategies.

- Information access

  - Prospectus – learning mentor (LM), LSU, Inclusion Team – access for pupils and parents.

  - Sharing information, confidentiality policy, common language.

  - Multi-agency databases.

  - Role of independent advice – Connexions services – role of class teacher, LM, and so on.

Support:

- Range of support available.

- Quality of support – monitoring of usage.

- Service Level Agreements with outside agencies.

- BEST, therapists and so an.

4. Curriculum

- Range of curriculum – providing whole range of life experiences – appropriate to individual needs – meet the requirements of *Every Child Matters* outcomes. Vocational, life skills and personalised learning as well as academic courses.

- Timetabling and flexibility – length of lessons.

- Curriculum pathways – using a mix and match approach.

- Extra-curricular activities – range of integrated activities, before, during and after school, and during summer holiday periods.

- Emphasis on key skills and personalised learning throughout early, primary, secondary and further education.

- Secondary – range of pathways, for example, Skill Force, ASDAN training providers (life skills programme); colleges/courses.

5. Learning and teaching

- Acknowledgement of a wide range of learning styles, for example, visual, sensory, practical – impact on those who have learning, behaviour and/or communication difficulties; gifted and talented.

- Need to be part of the identification process in order to better assess learning needs.

- Curriculum needs to reflect the range of learning styles, pupils' interests and needs.

- Poor teaching can lead to disengagement – need to look at ways to interest and excite pupils – engagement, communication and building relationships with learners are of paramount importance.

- Using complementary skills of all professionals in the teaching and learning processes.

- Setting pupils' targets – individual planning (IEPs, PSPs and so on). Monitoring pupils' rates of progress.

6. Effective transition

- Important milestones of pupils' lives.

- Internal sharing of information when pupils move from year to year.

- Involving all agencies.

- Learning mentors' role: induction; working with Key Stages 2 and 3 pupils; visits; helping pupils feel comfortable about the next stage of learning; meeting with staff and so on.

- Common and complementary protocols and practices including the transfer of documentation – agreed by all agencies.

- Roles of managers, key workers and lead professionals.

7. Management and training

- Need an inclusive management structure with a clear referral process to reflect the range of pupil barriers to learning.

- Develop skilled, multi-agency workforce.

- Train volunteers and governors as a local resource.

- Use of other professionals.

- Courses for parents and carers.

8. Monitoring, evaluation and accountability

- Tracking of pupils' progress.

- Target setting – within the school and on a multi-agency basis, for example, behaviour, attitude, attendance, attainment and so on.

- Which data to collect and how to collect/collate it. Use of quantative and qualitative data.

- Reporting and reviewing mechanisms.

- Using appropriate data to monitor trends, identify best practice and inform forward planning.

Key Principles underlying the strategy (to be set within the context of the school)

- A pupil-centred approach – needs of the pupil are at the heart of decision-making.

- A holistic, multi-agency, joined-up approach to inclusion to meet the needs of pupils.

- Ensuring best value in service delivery.

Outcomes

Include a range of outcomes/benefits that are expected to result from the successful implementation of the strategy, for example:

- a strategic and co-ordinated approach to inclusion

- better communication and joint working between agencies

- better and earlier identification of pupils' needs

- more effective transition

- higher attainment levels, attendance, improved punctuality and behaviour

- pupils feeling more positive about learning and about themselves as individuals

Resources

- Financial.

- IT and range of equipment.

- People.

- Partnership arrangements/outsourcing.

Implementation

- How the strategy will be implemented.

- Who are the key players?

- Annual implementation plans outlining key actions, timescales, milestones, resources and responsibilities.

- Ongoing monitoring, evaluation and review of the strategy to ensure it is meeting the desired outcomes/targets/benefits.

- Review, reporting and dissemination procedures.

Critical success factors

What are the essential factors if the strategy is to succeed? For example:

- good planning

- management commitment/direction

- sufficient resources and capacity

- ensuring the strategy and ensuing policies contribute clearly to the *Every Child Matters* key outcomes

- joined-up working

- excellent communication between all parties.

These headings are intended as a guide only and can be adapted to suit the particular circumstances of each school. The framework is a highly valuable tool to help structure thinking around the strategy development and to gain buy-in and commitment at an early stage of the process. Throughout the development of the strategy, it is essential to refer regularly to the outcomes framework of *Every Child Matters* to ensure the strategy focuses on the key outcomes.

Suggestions for making it happen ...

- 'Establish a strategy team with a leader/chairperson and representatives from staff, governors, agencies and pupils.

- Ensure that sufficient time is allocated and clear deadlines agreed – ideally a strategy should be completed within two terms and submitted to the governing body for approval.

- The strategy will involve extensive consultation with staff, pupils, parents and other stakeholders which will provide useful evidence for the completion of the school Self-Evaluation Form.

- The strategy should be practical, easy to read and regularly used. Personnel within the Inclusion Team should have a clear allocation of tasks. Displaying the strategy in the staff room and offices will help to focus and refer to areas during meetings.

- Use the thinking and evidence from the strategy to formulate the inclusion policy

Inclusion policies

Creating an inclusion policy takes time and thought. It needs to follow on from the development of the strategy – this will help structure the thinking and provide the evidence base for developing the policy. All staff, pupils and parents need to take ownership. There are a number of different approaches schools can take to developing inclusion policies. Some schools have a short overarching 'umbrella' policy with a series of detailed supporting policies. Others include everything within one detailed policy. Much depends on the nature, context and past practice of the school. Springwood Heath Primary School – an amalgamation of mainstream, primary and Special School in Liverpool has developed its own approach to developing an inclusive policy. The staff asked their school council what inclusion meant to them, in reply pupils stated 'inclusion is allowing everyone to do everything even if they are different'. Staff worked on very helpful ideas of what is an inclusive classroom with the following headings:

Basic Organisation

- All children are able to move and work in an orderly way.
- The space available is fully utilised.
- Classrooms have clearly defined curriculum areas, which the children are aware of.

- The organisation and labelling of resources encourages effective work.
- The classroom is fully prepared for the beginning of the session and cleared methodically at the end.
- Each classroom door is clearly labelled with the appropriate year group and teacher's name.

Classroom Display

- The children's work reflects planning and local and national interests.
- There is a balance between children's, teacher's and published materials.
- There is space available to display 3D items.
- Opportunities are made available for children to display their own chosen work.

Pupil Management

- Basic strategies are used to encourage children to gain team points, star awards and SMART [specific, measurable, achievable, realistic and timely] stamps.
- Each classroom is a friendly, stimulating secure place.
- Children are encouraged to learn how to organise their time and to prioritise their work tasks.

Management of Space
We prefer working in classrooms that allow:

- Freedom of movement
- Children to work together, as a whole class or by themselves in a variety of assignments
- Teacher able to address the whole class
- Safe display of work and resources
- Flexibility to vary activities from day to day or lesson to lesson, with the minimum of disruption. (Staff, Governors, children and parents of Springwood Heath Primary School)

Although this is for primary classrooms it is equally applicable and can be adapted to a secondary classroom setting. Discussion around this with staff will prove helpful for the Inclusion Team to get an insight into how individual staff plan and manage inclusion within their classroom. It can also be used as a training session which could ultimately form the basis of a school policy for classroom and lesson planning.

There are two good examples of policies/statements on the CD; see Chapter 3 Examples 2a–b.

In the light of the new Children's Services agenda, it would be useful to develop an inclusion policy around the five key outcomes of *Every Child Matters*:

- *Be healthy.*

- *Stay safe.*

- *Enjoy and achieve.*

- *Make a positive contribution.*

- *Achieve economic well-being.*

As these *Every Child Matters* five key outcomes will drive future inspections, services and provision it makes sense to start developing policies and practices around these areas. This will also help to develop a common framework for discussions with multidisciplinary professionals and common links with other Children's Services structures. Every local authority will develop structures around these five outcomes.

The following is a suggested approach to putting the inclusion policy under the five key outcomes (see CD, Chapter 3 Example 3):

Be healthy

To ensure all pupils try to be healthy, the school has:

- adopted healthy school standard awards

- carried our risk assessments on all appropriate pupils and information shared with staff

- developed a range of activities, provision and skills (some purchased) which encourages healthy, emotional and physical well-being, and assessment of pupils' physical, sexual and emotional health is a key part of the overall assessment process

- support for those pupils who are at risk of pregnancy or who have had an abortion, and work takes place with all pupils on sexual and mental health and positive relationships

- information and activities for parents and pupils about healthy lifestyles

- for pupils with long-term health conditions, co-ordinated quality services which allow them and their families to live as ordinary lives as possible

- work/policies on drug addiction/alcoholism in place along with strategies to reduce dependency, and there is extended work with outside agencies and organisations

- support for pupils with a range of barriers which affect mental and emotional health, such as young carers, pupils who move frequently, those from disengaged families and from families who have a disregard for education

- strong multi-agency links (CAMHS, Education Welfare Service – EWS, health and social services).

Stay safe

To help all pupils stay safe, the school has:

- an Inclusion Team with clear areas of responsibility with respect to child protection and advice and guidance on disclosures and sharing information, and that child protection arrangements meet the requirements of *Working Together to Safeguard Children* guidance DfES, 2006

- training in place for all staff and those from other agencies on how to recognise and raise child protection concerns, and training needs are regularly reviewed

- a clearly understood confidentiality policy which is agreed by all agencies working with schools

- effective and well co-ordinated links with other agencies through the Inclusion Team and panels (EWS, Youth Offending Team, social services, police, health, voluntary sector, support staff and so on)

- worked with parents on developing safe environments for children

- supported those pupils who are 'looked after' to stay safe and achieve their potential

- induction programmes for new and supply staff on aspects of staying safe within the school environment, including discrimination

- clear guidance within the school and the Inclusion Team on recording information, particularly those pupils identified to be at risk and those pupils who move frequently within and outside the local area

- a curriculum and extended activities which encourage safe and positive play and a peaceful playground environment

- work with multi-agencies such as the police, Youth Offending Team and Sure Start on staying safe in the local community.

Enjoy and achieve

To ensure all pupils enjoy and achieve, the school has:

- early years provision which prepares children for school and helps them to meet early learning goals

- support for parents and carers in helping their children to enjoy and achieve

- effective early identification and assessment of any barriers to learning strategies are in place

- systems of referral, and locates information on school inclusion databases

- a range of IEP support plans available

- regular assessment which is used to plan future work and help pupils understand how they can improve

- induction for pupils that takes into account the full range of their needs

- targets which are set for pupils with a range of needs, and teachers with high expectations

- pupils making good progress in relation to their starting points

- pupils achieving in line with those pupils with similar difficulties and circumstances

- a range of support available (SEN, LSU, LMs, counsellors, therapists and so on) to support learning and have impact on achievement

- support for transfer and transition in place

- effective quality assurance systems in place to ensure greatest impact possible

- staff who know and understand the needs of the range of pupils with barriers to learning and understand practical strategies for meeting these needs in the classroom

- suitable resources that are used to enable pupils to access the curriculum

- a curriculum which is matched to pupils' needs and is enjoyable

- pupils whose attendance is good (above 92 percent) and unauthorised absence is low

- fixed and permanent exclusions which are low, and strategies are in place to ensure a proactive response

- strategies in place throughout the school to improve attendance – roles of attendance officer, pastoral teams, class teachers, learning mentors, education welfare officers are clear – and training for meeting the needs of pupils and the range of strategies needed is in place for all staff

- personalised learning programmes including family learning activities.

Make a positive contribution

To make a positive contribution, the school has:

- a proactive, consistently applied, effective whole-school management policy promoting positive behaviour

- clear tracking systems which monitor behaviour, type, frequency, locations and time of day – which in turn will influence policy

- parents who are partners in this process with pupils and key members of staff

- behaviour and attendance consultants who are actively involved with the school and there are a range of resources such as time-out rooms, learning support units, counsellors, therapists and learning mentors to support pupils with a range of behaviour, social, emotional and mental health issues

- opportunities for all pupils to learn about disability issues

- a policy on bullying with peer mentoring schemes to support those pupils at risk

- pupils who are included in a range of extended curriculum and inclusion opportunities and activities

- pupils who participate in part-time/flexible mainstream placement activities

- an active approach to personal and social development

■ pupils achieving a range of accreditation in personal development and work/employment skills, through ASDAN, Ed excel certificates, working for life modules, independence, work and living skills

■ pupils who are actively encouraged to discuss and contribute to IEPs and reviews, and their opinions are used in shaping new provision and evaluating current practice

■ equality and diversity statements that impact on practice

■ learning mentors who develop a range of activities, for example, circle of friends, anti-bullying, positive behaviour management, bereavement and anger management work

■ pupils that are active members of the student council

■ support for pupils and their families at key transition stages.

Achieve economic well-being

To achieve economic well-being, the school has …

■ specialist support and help for those pupils whose academic achievement, particularly in key skills, falls below their peers

■ a curriculum which is reviewed regularly in the light of regular audits of pupils' needs and feedback; programmes are established either in school or other settings such as colleges, training providers, discrete curriculum groups and so on, alternative education programmes, aim higher, and so on

■ effective quality assurance mechanisms in place with colleges and various training providers; establishment of clear tracking procedures to ensure that pupils are achieving targets and making sufficient progress

■ a curriculum which provides a range of work/vocational courses and experiences for the full range of pupils, that is, NVQ levels 1, 2, and 3, GNVQ, targets set for percentage of students achieving work, college, training provider placements, and access/participate in the Duke of Edinburgh Award Scheme

■ pupils who achieve their potential with regard to examination success and qualifications

■ pupils who have a range of effective support that increases motivation, aspirations and study skills through support/revision programmes

■ worked in conjunction with external agencies and parents that help pupils to be economically active and self-sustaining

■ quality progression planning, possibly in conjunction with Connexions/careers advisers, to support effective planning and dialogue

■ a 14–19 strategy which helps those pupils supported by the Inclusion Team to prepare for working life and acquire team working and effective communication skills.

Suggestions for making it happen ...

- Allocate time, leadership and membership of the team developing the policy.

- Look at a range of policy approaches which could suit the school.

- The policy should be clearly linked to the *Every Child Matters* key outcomes.

- Consultation should build on that undertaken for the strategy.

- Once complete, the policy should be disseminated and publicised.

- It is essential that the inclusion policy is:

  - reviewed regularly

  - updated when needed

  - shared with all staff

  - integrated into other whole-school policies and subject/department policies/strategies

  - informed by feedback from staff, pupils, carers and agencies

  - a core part of induction and other training for a wide range of staff

  - supported by a series of detailed specific policies

  - integrated into the Self-Evaluation Form (SEF) as part of the ongoing evaluation process.

- Creating a policy is only part of the creation of a fully inclusive school – the other elements are:

  - creation of inclusive cultures

  - building the school as a community

  - establishing inclusive values

  - evolving inclusive practices which facilitate learning for all and best use of resources to enable this to happen. A useful inclusion action plan is included on the CD, Chapter 3 Example 4.

Inclusion models

As a result of the move towards a more inclusive school and widening SEN to encompass a wide range of pupils with barriers to learning, the staffing structures and models by which inclusion services are delivered have changed.

Historically SEN services were delivered through:

- the special educational needs co-ordinator (SENCO)

- a team of teaching assistants

- educational psychologists.

- LEA support services – such as learning support, behavioural support, support for pupils with physical/sensory difficulties, support for pupils from ethnic minority backgrounds

- a range of therapists – for example, speech and language, art, drama, music.

INCLUSION MANAGER/ SENCO	KEY STAGE MANAGERS	LSU/ NURTURE GROUP	LEARNING MENTORS	TEACHING ASSISTANTS
Overall responsibility for co-ordination. Multi-agency involvement and allocation of resources through inclusion panel.	Tracking pupils and monitoring progress. Judging whether sufficient progress is being made.	Outreach support and in-house provision for pupils with emotional/ behavioural difficulties.	Either attached to Key Stages or have general caseload across the school.	Attached to key States target key pupils – statemented and vulnerable

Figure 3.1   General Inclusion Model for a primary school (Depending on size)

With the expansion of the inclusion agenda, a whole new team is formed encompassing support for pupils with a wide range of needs, including mental health, some of which will be short term, others ongoing. In addition, the number of initiatives, programmes and agencies has expanded dramatically over the past six years. These have to be found a 'home' so that there is no duplication of the role and that best value is gained from the resource. There have also been a number of funding routes entering the school which naturally fall into the inclusion agenda. Co-ordination has become a challenge and the key to the success of the inclusion programme in schools.

Key factors to consider when developing inclusion models, both in primary and secondary schools are:

- review staffing structures and roles

- ensure that there are clear decision-making routes

- communication should flow and information be easily retrievable

- the development of an inclusion panel that will look at referrals, those pupils who are currently supported and the allocation of resources

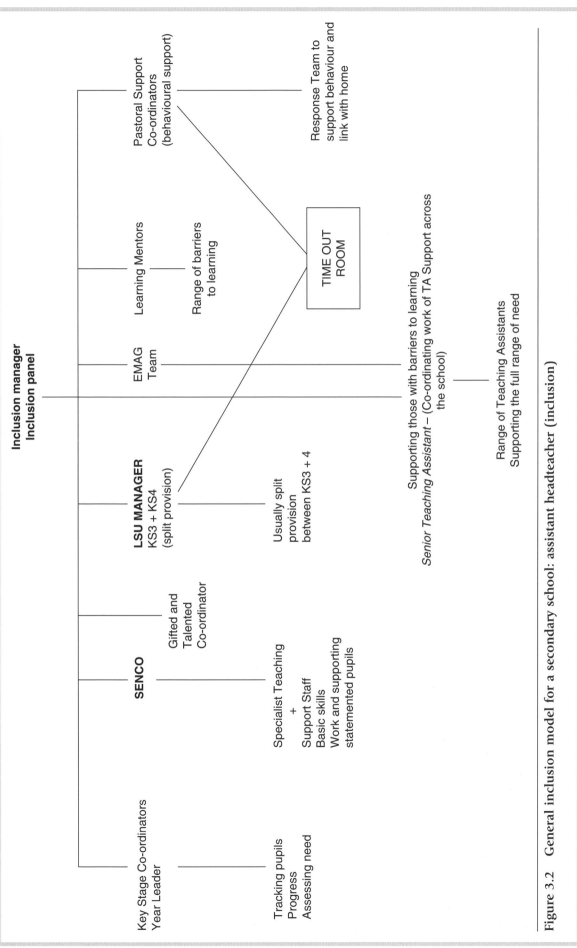

**Inclusion manager
Inclusion panel**

Key Stage Co-ordinators
Year Leader

Tracking pupils
Progress
Assessing need

SENCO

Gifted and
Talented
Co-ordinator

Specialist Teaching
+
Support Staff
Basic skills
Work and supporting
statemented pupils

LSU MANAGER
KS3 + KS4
(split provision)

Usually split
provision
between KS3 + 4

EMAG
Team

Learning Mentors

Range of barriers
to learning

Pastoral Support
Co-ordinators
(behavioural support)

Response Team to
support behaviour and
link with home

TIME OUT
ROOM

Supporting those with barriers to learning
Senior Teaching Assistant – (Co-ordinating work of TA Support across
the school)

Range of Teaching Assistants
Supporting the full range of need

Figure 3.2   General inclusion model for a secondary school: assistant headteacher (inclusion)

- consistent and complementary action planning which does not lead to duplication

- clear strategies for tracking pupils and the impact of services that are provided for them.

Practical steps to develop an appropriate inclusion model include:

- brainstorming the range of support that is available and the range of services that the school provides

- identifying key areas of strengths and where the gaps are

- assessing and having knowledge of the amount of funding coming into the school from various services, that is, EIC, BIP, BEST, Sure Start, SEN, Ethnic Minority Achievement Grant (EMAG), school budget

- identifying the barriers to learning and range of needs entering the school.

The model created should have an impact on:

- more effective deployment of support in the classroom

- greater stability and sustainability of the provision

- creating more permanent contracts for staff

- creating better planning time for staff before and after school.

Inclusion panels and referral process

One of the key features of the inclusion model is the inclusion panel and systems of referral to and from it. The key features of an effective inclusion panel are as follows:

- Meetings on a regular basis with time allocated for key members of staff to attend; these should be timetabled on a yearly wall planner throughout the year.

- there is a chairperson, an agenda circulated well in advance, and minutes taken and fed back directly after the meeting.

- Referrals to the panel need to be on a single referral form – this will cover referrals for learning, behaviour and any other 'additional support' that is needed. They must be completed in a consistent and informed way by staff.

- In small schools, referrals can go directly to the inclusion panel if it meets regularly. In larger schools it may be better to have a 'filter system' in order that the Inclusion Panel does not get swamped with inappropriate referrals. In this case, there could be separate weekly meetings with pastoral support managers/Connexions/education welfare officer/LSU/student support service/learning mentor to address clearly identifiable behaviour/attendance needs, with another meeting involving SENCO/pastoral manager/ learning mentor with respect to those pupils on the SEN Code of Practice. Therefore referrals to the full inclusion panel are those pupils with more complex needs.

- There is also a place for pupil self-referral. In the first instance, these might go to the learning mentor or through a peer mentoring programme.

- The inclusion panel will have a range of referral routes it can make including:

  - learning mentor and peer mentoring

  - student support centre/learning support centre

  - PRU

  - full statutory assessment

  - Connexions services

  - withdrawal groups.

  - range of Key Stage 4 alternative provision

  - gifted and talented co-ordinator

  - specific language/literacy support

  - behaviour team.

  - family work

  - Youth Offending Team

  - range of extended activities, before and after school, holiday activities

  - counselling

  - therapy – drama, music, art

  - range of projects in the community

  - refugee support.

The list will become endless. The challenge is to co-ordinate and ensure that the services have a positive impact on the pupil. The inclusion panel is also a facility where cases can be brought back for a professional debate after insufficient or no progress has been made. The panel can also give advice to staff on inappropriate referrals and strategies to improve the situation. See CD, Chapter 3 Examples 5a–b for two approaches to referral systems.

Challenges of models

There are real challenges involved in establishing inclusion models and systems. In the main these can include the following:

- Some staff find change difficult and therefore resist and become territorial.

- Especially in large schools, there will be a number of staff who have particular ways of circumnavigating systems by the 'back door'. Senior managers are very adept at this and need to follow agreed practice and policy, particularly on a Friday afternoon when the LSU is full.

- Models need to be sufficiently flexible to respond effectively to crises when they occur, but this must not take the place of a planned approach to resources or provision. This is particularly an issue with pupils who have behaviour, emotional and mental health difficulties.

- As schools are dealing with such a wide range of agencies, there will be a host of different referral systems and protocols from these agencies. The challenge is to try and have common/complementary procedures to avoid duplication. The multi-agency databases and the Common Assessment Framework being established between education, health and social services will help improve access to information and regulate systems.

- Staff need to understand that the Inclusion Team are not miracle workers. There are pupils who have such deep-rooted problems which need such specialist support that they cannot survive in mainstream schools. Learning support units cannot change behaviour overnight. Some staff feel that there should be an immediate change on exit, rather like pupils taking a pill which makes them a different person. As inclusion is a process, so is the way which the services impact on pupils. Pupils' difficulties could be as a result of a range of problems such as:

  - inappropriate curriculum

  - poor teacher–pupil and pupil–pupil relationships

  - inappropriate teaching strategies

  - unhappiness about themselves.

Therefore with many pupils, it may take some time to work through and solve problems. It will also take diplomatic tenacity on the part of the Inclusion Team to challenge certain members of staff whose reply about changing styles or ways of working is that 'I have always done it that way'. This is why one of the most crucial elements to making this happen is the support, vision and 'clout' of the Senior Leadership Team.

Suggestions for making it happen ...

- Research a range of models/referral processes/documentation in order to determine which best meets the needs within the school.

- Inclusion panels are essential to co-ordinate and allocate/review resources and must therefore be given regular meeting times during the school day. Cover will need to be arranged.

- The inclusion panel will need to be clear about the entry and exit criteria of the range of resources in order to make appropriate referrals and obtain best value.

Inclusion training

With the wealth of experience, knowledge and qualifications, and the diverse nature of staff within Inclusion Teams, planning a training/professional development programme is a challenge and a key role in itself. In essence, professional development and training needs to be planned for the following groups:

■ Inclusion Team staff

■ whole-school staff – teachers, teaching assistants, senior managers, lunchtime staff, administrative staff, caretaking and maintenance staff

■ Multi-agency professionals – services from health, social services, range of outside links/voluntary groups

■ governors and parents/carers.

The most important element of this training is its impact on pupils' attainment, achievement, attitude and so on, and the progress that they make. This is a difficult concept to measure accurately, however, if the training programme is targeted and driven by the inclusion strategy and policy, then it is more likely to be able to be measured in terms of outcomes. In essence, best practice shows that training is most effective when it is:

■ part of an overall professional development programme

■ based on a clear audit and analysis of needs

■ part of a nationally recognised accreditation process

■ built on prior education, learning, knowledge and experience

■ flexible enough to meet the changing needs of the pupil population

■ planned and delivered within a multi-agency framework

■ recognised and valued by staff

■ given high priority and time/support is allocated.

A professional development programme goes well beyond staff attending courses. Opportunities for professional development could include:

■ access to networking meetings – both learning mentors and learning support unit managers will have support groups and information-sharing activities

■ visiting other schools to observe and share practice – this is invaluable for the professional concerned and can be targeted at specific areas; some learning support unit managers and learning mentors have used this time as an opportunity to 'audit' each other using the audit tools

■ shadowing other staff in schools – one of the challenges of working in an Inclusion Team is the range of different roles involved. Shadowing can improve understanding and inform practice. Some staff in schools view 'inclusion support' as 'swanning around' as many of the staff are dealing with one-to-one cases or small groups. Sharing case studies, attending briefing meetings and having a section of the staffroom notice board giving information on pupils are all useful strategies to improve understanding of the different roles.

In addition to formal training, the school will need to work with individuals and organisations within the local community to raise awareness of the school's approach to inclusion, to involve the community more in the life of the school and to consider how the school can support the community, for example, through Extended School provision and Sure Start children's centre. Similarly, community organisations will need to consider how they, in turn, can support the school's inclusion agenda.

Induction

Induction is an integral part of the training and professional development process for all staff in the Inclusion Team. Opportunities should be given to:

- talk to key members of staff about the school and their role

- talk to groups and individual pupils

- observe around the school – in class, during break, lunchtimes, before and after school – to gain an understanding of the school's routines

- work with the line manager and other key staff such as the SENCO, learning support unit manager and attendance officer on identifying pupils who are underachieving; this will involve the use of data and analysis of trends

- understanding referral arrangements, criteria for referral, assessment strategies and so on

- agreeing operational procedures such as attending meetings, how to collect data (if appropriate) and monitoring and evaluation procedures

- agreeing caseloads as appropriate and target groups of pupils.

Aspiring inclusion workers

There are also courses that may be useful for people wanting to join the Inclusion Team. Examples of courses that aspiring inclusion workers have found useful have been those on:

- counselling skills and techniques

- emotional, behavioural and social difficulties

- emotional literacy

- anger management

- circle time

- working one to one or in groups

- youth work and social work

- working with families

- working with other agencies and understanding their roles.

The choice of the most appropriate training and development will also depend on the preferred area of work and the context of the school, that is, early years, primary, special, secondary, further education or specific programmes such as those for asylum seekers or pupils who move frequently, looked after children or those in pupil referral units.

Accredited training

There are a number of accredited training programmes emerging to support professionals working within the Inclusion Team. The main thrust is one of ensuring that the *Every Child Matters* five key outcomes, and the skills and knowledge associated with them, are effectively incorporated into training and support systems for the Children's Workforce. One of the key features of any training is the multidisciplinary approach and the importance of involving a range of disciplines in the delivery.

National Occupational Standards

National Occupational Standards (NOS) were first developed in 1980s as a response to improving vocational education training qualifications. In essence, they:

- are based on current best practice and future practice development

- break tasks down into identified outcomes

- are capable of reliable, objective and consistent assessment across the UK, with a real emphasis on the use of evidence from actual working practices.

These standards then inform the content of National Vocational Qualification (NVQ) systems and other qualifications. There are a wide range of National Occupational Standards, many of which are relevant to the education service, that is early years workers, play workers, youth workers and so on.

The National Occupational Standards for Learning Development and Support Services for Children, Young People and those who care for them were developed by analysing the work of learning mentors, education welfare officers and Connexions advisers. The standards are presented as a series of units of competence relating to specific roles. A skilled and competent practitioner is defined as working at level 4 with a less experienced practitioner, or 'trainee', being expected to operate initially at level 3. Level 4 shows recognition of the level of complexity and responsibility undertaken in posts such as these. For more details see website www.dfes.gov.uk/childrenandfamilies/nos.shtml.

The DfES expects the NOS to be used in a variety of ways. Perhaps the most important is their potential in workforce development in ensuring that service provision is of an appropriate standard. Employers can use them as a yardstick for measuring standards of practice, as an element of performance management/appraisal procedures as well as setting a framework for professional development. The human resources related uses are also significant – standards can clearly be used in constructing job descriptions and person specifications, and they are useful in assisting services to devise recruitment strategies. This is particularly helpful when creating new posts such as student/pupil support workers which are being developed through initiatives such as School Workforce Reform.

These standards can be used across the Inclusion Team and provide a framework for the professional development and training programme. In addition, there is more specific training for teaching assistants and higher level teaching assistants. Learning mentors have an initial five-day training programme which is delivered locally through the learning mentor co-ordinator, who also delivers a range of training programmes specific to individual and school needs. For more details about learning mentor training see website www.standard.DfES.gov.uk/excellence/policies/mentors and for teaching assistants, website www.teachernet.gov.uk/wholeschool/teachingassistants.

Training in behaviour and attendance is being led nationally through the National Programme for Specialist Leaders of Behaviour and Attendance. The programme offers qualifications and creates career pathways for the growing number of specialists who work in the field of behaviour and attendance. Not all of these professionals are teachers. They work in varied settings: in mainstream primary or secondary schools, in Special Schools or units, and as LEA officers. The programme is organised and delivered by a team of regional co-ordinators within the Improving Behaviour and Attendance Unit of the DfES, providing training opportunities in the nine government regions. There is a co-ordinator in each region who can be contacted for details – see end of chapter for details. It is envisaged that the programme will train a minimum of 3,500 behaviour and attendance professionals per year and there is a growing interest from those leading multi-agency teams and other aspects of the *Every Child Matters* agenda. The programme has a broad set of learning materials, which can be tailored to the individual professional's needs and their own capacity for study. The first unit concentrates on inclusion and has a very useful index which can be used with staff. This makes the programme accessible for a wide range of staff and gives them a career path to follow. Support will also be given to those working in learning support units through regional support officers who are practitioners able to be released to work and train alongside staff in schools.

From September 2005, the Teacher Training Agency (TTA) became the Training and Development Agency for Schools (TDA), with additional responsibilities for the entire school workforce. Until then, no single organisation had responsibilities for the training and development of teachers and support staff.

Whole-school training including governors

One of the key roles of the inclusion co-ordinator/manager and the Inclusion Team will be to facilitate whole-school training for the full range of staff working in schools. The most effective training is that which addresses practical issues. Staff can relate to these and see the relevance and application. A useful starting point is to:

- look at the various barriers to learning entering the school

- audit the level of need

- use a number of case studies within the school to highlight the various barriers to learning. This could be done as an exercise with Governors. Case studies from the DfES website for learning mentors or learning support units would be a good start if there are no studies readily available. The following are two examples of case study scenarios which could be helpful in getting staff/governors and others to:

- identify needs that are not being catered for

- identify the range of support that is available

- develop and implement the most appropriate support programme.

Mary

Mary is an only child living with her single mum. She is in year 4. She has difficulty building relationships with her peers and other children, and plays on her own in the playground. She does not want to sit with the other children during activities in the classroom, for example, during storytelling and group activities.

Mary has learning difficulties and is behind in her class.

Mary's mum came to the school when Mary had a tantrum and had to be carried out of the classroom after causing a scene in front of the other pupils, screaming, kicking the teacher and spitting. When Mary was taken out of the classroom and seated in the waiting area for her mum she started to bang her head against the wall.

Pedro

Pedro and his parents came to the UK eight months ago following a period of political unrest in their homeland. Pedro's father now works as a road-sweeper and his mother rarely leaves the home.

Pedro is in year 9, very bright, and his English is improving. He never has friends round to the house and is conscious of how lonely his mother is and always goes straight home after school to help with the housework and shopping. His mother does not speak English and relies on Pedro to communicate for her. Some of the boys in his year have targeted Pedro saying he is a mummy's boy and is gay. Their interest in him is becoming out of hand with aggressive behaviour, bullying and threatening tactics.

It is important to:

- encourage discussion and working groups where possible

- mix the various groups of staff together, that is, support staff, teaching assistants, teachers, Inclusion Team members, governors and senior managers, but also build in opportunities for these groups to meet on their own so that they can share and feel safe with close colleagues

- have ideas and strategies to meet the varying needs through effective teaching and learning

- look at the impact of inclusion support on individual pupils through case studies with a focus on pupils' achievement and progress in a number of areas. This will help staff to see the impact of home and other circumstances on attitude, motivation in class and attainment.

Also, case studies can be useful for intray exercises during interviews. These will give the interviewing panel a good idea of approaches and attitudes that potential staff might take.

The DfES Primary National Strategy includes Leading on Inclusion training material for staff in primary schools, but the framework can also be used for secondary schools. This material can be downloaded from the DfES Standards website www.standards.dfes.gov.uk.

Suggestions for making it happen ...

- Training should be clearly linked to the school's inclusion strategy and policy.

- There needs to be a range of training, that is, induction, ongoing whole-school development and training specific to the professionals in the Inclusion Team.

- Resources need to be allocated in terms of:

    - finance

    - time

    - access to consultants

- Training is not just about courses – it can also involve:

    - shadowing peers

    - visiting other schools

    - network meetings.

Bringing it all together – key features of an inclusive school

It is often difficult to measure your progress in moving to an inclusive school. An OFSTED survey of provision for different types of SEN identified the following key characteristics of effective, inclusive schools (*Special educational needs in the mainstream* – OFSTED, 2003):

- a climate of acceptance of all pupils, including those who have distinctive needs

- careful planning of placements for pupils with SEN, giving attention to the pupils themselves, their peers in school, parents and staff

- the availability of sufficient suitable teaching and personal support

- widespread awareness among staff of the particular needs of pupils and understanding of practical ways of meeting them in classrooms and elsewhere

- sensitive allocation to teaching groups and careful modification of the curriculum, timetables and social arrangements

- the availability of appropriate materials and teaching aids and adapted accommodation

- an active approach to personal and social development, as well as to learning

- well-defined and consistently applied approaches to managing difficult behaviour

- assessment, recording and reporting procedures which can embrace and express adequately the progress of pupils who may make only small gains in learning and personal development

- involving parents as fully as possible in decision-making, keeping them well informed about their child's progress and giving them as much practical support as possible

- developing and taking advantage of training opportunities, including links with special schools and other schools providing for similar group of pupils with SEN.

The report also concludes that almost all schools needed effective external support from local authority and other services in order to:

- obtain sufficient, timely and coherent help from specialist teachers, therapists, psychologists, medical staff and social workers

- create a suitable and efficient learning environment

- regularly monitor placements to ensure that they are meeting the needs of pupils as well as possible

- improve the assessment arrangement so that there is a clear statement of the sometimes changing nature of a child's special needs linked to the implications for learning

- extend the training opportunities available to ensure that school staff are well informed and confident about teaching pupils with a range of learning, emotional, behavioural and social difficulties

- benefit from connections with special schools in terms of guidance, training, resources and the monitoring of progress.

These key characteristics can provide a useful checklist for schools (see the CD, Chapter 3 Example 6) in measuring how far they have progressed towards developing an inclusive school. There are a number of useful checklists and inclusion standards that schools can use to help establish and review inclusive practices: for example, Inclusion Standard – High Standards for All – Manchester Education Department, www.manchester.gov.uk/education, and Index for Inclusion, www.inclusion.org.uk and www.csie.org.uk. It is also important to remember that working in isolation is not an option – all schools need the involvement and support of the local authority, special schools and services, statutory, voluntary and other agencies if their school is to become truly inclusive.

Look It Up ...

- National Programme for Specialist Leaders of Behaviour and Attendance. www.teachernet. gov.uk/npslba

- Foundation degree in working with young people and young people's services, Leeds Metropolitan University (Learning Mentors), www.lmu.ac.uk

- Governor training, www.teachernet.gov.uk/management/atoz/g/Governor_training/

- Safeguarding Children – Safe Recruitment and Selection in Education Settings (DfES, 2005), www.teachernet.gov.uk/childprotection

- Children's Workforce Development Council, www.cwdcouncil.org.uk

Managers and Management Matters

This chapter looks at the importance of good management of the inclusion agenda. Once you have your inclusion strategy and policy in place, you then need to manage their implementation systematically and effectively if they are to make an impact on pupils. This involves establishing clear roles and responsibilities for governors and senior managers and establishing and recruiting an effective Inclusion Team – basically, getting the right people. We look at the variety of roles involved in inclusion, including the new roles emerging from the *Every Child Matters* agenda. We also consider the management systems and processes which need to be in place if inclusion is to make a real difference.

The role of inclusion manager, assistant headteacher (inclusion), curriculum leader for SEN/ inclusion or the headteacher in a small school is a considerable one, which involves the effective management of a wide range of resources in order to maximise impact on pupils. Not for the fainthearted.

The Inclusion Team will be the most complex and varied in the whole school in terms of experience, knowledge, qualifications, roles and future aspirations. With the reforms in Children's Services and the new workforce and training strategies, the team will be able to work through this massive change agenda.

Vision and strategic planning are imperative to make inclusion happen and to achieve successful outcomes for all pupils. The vision must come from the governing body and Senior Leadership Team in order to provide strategic direction and inspiration for all those involved in the inclusion agenda.

Members of the Inclusion Team could be:

- inclusion manager

- SENCO

- LSU manager

- learning mentors

- education welfare officers

- education psychologists

- representatives from support services – sessional/part-time workers

- therapists – speech and language, occupational, physiotherapy, art, music, drama

- counsellors

- nurses/medical support

- pastoral support workers.

Role of the governing body

The governing body has a clear role in terms of strategy, accountability and as a 'critical friend' to the school and its managers. It is important that there is a governor for inclusion rather than SEN – the role has widened, and so should governor responsibilities. The role of governor for inclusion and of the governing body comprises the following.

Strategy

- Develop with the inclusion manager and the team the inclusion strategy and policy.

- Inform the governing body of the strategy and policy, and their responsibilities within these.

- Keep abreast of Children's Services developments and the new programmes/initiatives/ responsibilities which the school needs to meet its statutory duties.

- Be aware of the needs of the local community and how the school can meet these in part/whole.

- Ensure that there is a standing agenda item on inclusion developments and their impact on pupils' attainment and achievement.

- Be aware of the inclusion policy statement from the local authority.

Accountability

- The governing body needs to be aware of and to understand the needs of pupils entering the school with 'barriers to learning', and the impact that this will have on their achievement and progress.

- The governor for inclusion should prepare, in consultation with the governing body, information to assist the compilation of the school Self-Evaluation Form (SEF).

- Ensure that the views of parents, pupils and the local community are enshrined in the SEF and acted upon where appropriate.

- Governors should be involved in regular reviews and updates of the SEF.

■ Governors must have knowledge of the overall school budget and ensure that the budget allocated for inclusion is sufficient and targeted in appropriate ways so that it offers best value in terms of outcome and quality.

Critical friend

■ Be available to work with the Inclusion Team on aspects of the development of provision and attend training opportunities.

■ The governor for inclusion should use the experience and expertise of the governing body and local community to challenge and support the work of the Inclusion Team and the school as a whole.

■ The governing body as a whole works to ensure that the inclusion agenda permeates every aspect of the school's work.

Governors clearly play an important role in the inclusion agenda and schools need to ensure that governors are appointed with the appropriate skills and experience, and that they receive ongoing training and support in order to fulfil their duties.

Role of the Senior Management/Leadership Team

This team must be the cornerstone for the success and positive outcome of the inclusion strategy and policy. The role will vary depending on the context and size of the school. However, the key principles of the role with respect to strategic inclusion are:

■ providing the strategic lead and 'clout' across the school and local community to ensure the effective inclusion of families and pupils into the school

■ to ensure that the inclusion strategy and policy are embedded in all aspects of the school's work, including meeting legal requirements

■ to ensure that the school meets the Children's Services agenda, *Every Child Matters* and incorporates multidisciplinary working as a key part of its ethos and culture

■ that the allocation of monies to promote and deliver the inclusion agenda, including the statutory requirements of those pupils with statements, are sufficient and that they provide best value for pupils in terms of the quality of service

■ To ensure that resources – physical, human and financial – are clearly targeted to pupil need, and that there are regular reviews of this, with appropriate changes made

■ that pupils' needs, attainment, achievement and outcomes are tracked across the school to ensure that the progress they make is sufficient and matched to their potential

■ to ensure that the inclusion agenda quality assurance and review process are reflected in the school Self-Evaluation Form or equivalent document.

Establishing the Inclusion Team

Once the vision and strategic direction are agreed, the team-building can begin. Clearly, the team will play a significant part in the development and implementation of the inclusion strategy and policy. However, it needs to have clear strategic direction from the 'top' in order to develop and implement effective practice.

Building an effective team with a diverse group of people in terms of experience, knowledge, understanding, wide skill base, qualifications and aspirations is an exciting challenge. The following is a useful checklist.

An effective team:

- shares the vision and agreed goals

- has a climate of support and trust

- has open lines of communication

- recognises that conflict is inevitable and can be constructive

- has clear direction

- has leadership appropriate to its membership

- reviews its progress regularly

- is concerned with the development of its members

- relates positively to other groups.

The team will have a variety of strengths and skills, which may well change and develop as the team matures. A particularly useful exercise in understanding the character and type of each team member each is that of Belbin. This exercise looks at the different roles people play in teams, and describes each role along with the associated weaknesses. Staff complete a questionnaire which, when analysed, gives a score and the range of team roles they can perform – most people can undertake more that one role.

The following is an illustration of Belbin Team Worker roles adapted from *Team Management: Why Management Teams Succeed or Fail* (Belbin – Heinemann, 1981).

The assumption behind the role mix is that successful teams contain at least one person able to undertake each of the nine roles, and that team members can switch roles depending on the context. It is also a useful tool to help decide who should attend meetings. If you want someone to stir things up and generate action, then send a shaper or plant. If there is a need to see a detailed piece of work through, while maintaining good relations and diplomacy, then choose an implementer or a co-ordinator. This approach also provides managers and team members with ideas on future professional development for staff needing and wanting to develop differing roles. Further details on the process and access to Belbin questionnaires can be obtained by visiting www.belbin.com.

ROLES AND DESCRIPTIONS/ TEAM ROLE CONTRIBUTIONS	ALLOWABLE WEAKNESSES
IMPLEMENTER Disciplined, reliable, conservative and efficient. Turns ideas into practical actions.	Somewhat inflexible, slow to respond to new possibilities.
CO-ORDINATOR Mature, confident and trusting. A good chairman. Clarifies goals, promotes decision-making.	Not necessarily the most clever or creative member of a group.
SHAPER Dynamic, outgoing, highly strung. Challenges, pressurises, finds ways round obstacles.	Prone to provocation and short-lived bursts of temper.
PLANT Creative, imaginative, unorthodox. Solves difficult problems.	Weak in communicating with and managing people.
RESOURCE INVESTIGATOR Extrovert, enthusiastic, communicative. Explores opportunities. Develops contacts.	Loses interest once initial enthusiasm has passed.
MONITOR EVALUATOR Sober, strategic and discerning. Sees all options. Judges accurately.	Lacks drive and ability to inspire others.
TEAM WORKER Social, mild, perceptive and accommodating. Listens, builds, averts friction.	Indecisive in crunch situations.
COMPLETER FINISHER Painstaking, conscientious, anxious. Searches out errors and omissions. Delivers on time.	Inclined to worry unduly. Reluctant to delegate.
SPECIALIST Single minded, self-starting, dedicated. Provides knowledge and skills in rare supply	Contributes only on a narrow front. Dwells on technicalities.

Reproduced with permission from Belbin Associates.

Making the team work

The variety of roles and the huge complexity of needs facing schools present an exciting challenge when addressing roles and areas of responsibility. Inevitably there are going to be areas of overlap, duplication and, sometimes, conflict. With such a diverse range of disciplines and experience, it is essential that managers consider how the roles fit together so that the school and pupils get best value.

Some key principles

- There needs to be a clear understanding of the range of roles and functions of the members of the team, and their relationship with each other and with other professionals inside and outside the school.

- Roles and functions should not be restrictive – it is important to allow professional expertise and knowledge to develop in an open, non-competitive approach which is pupil focused.

- A co-ordinated approach to deployment of time and resources should be developed which is based on the needs of identified pupils.

- Flexibility is the key.

- The roles should be based within a clear management framework.

In practice, there can be tensions between roles. Past experience has shown that tensions can arise between the roles and areas of responsibility of learning mentors and teaching assistants, therapists and counsellors, and Connexions personal advisers and learning mentors. Some of these roles are new and, if they are not carefully managed, there can be misunderstandings about their function. This was particularly the case when learning mentors were first introduced into schools; staff were so relieved to have another 'body' in school that they gave them huge numbers of referrals, many of which were totally inappropriate.

A useful strategy to overcome this is to examine the roles and the main focus of work. Then, in order to see how roles fit together, place them under the following headings, listing features which are:

- common to other roles

- complementary to other roles – that is, activities may be separate but form part of a coherent framework of support for pupils

- distinctive areas – illustrating some clear differences in deployment.

This exercise can be undertaken with all the roles within an Inclusion Team or specifically with those that work closely together. It will also give greater clarity to the entire staff about the rationale for deployment and focus of the role. This is particularly important when new roles are emerging such as lead professionals, pastoral support managers and, even, inclusion managers.

The following is an example of the process in practice, looking at learning mentors and Connexions personal advisers.

Learning Mentor – focus of work

- Emphasis on pupils between years 7 and 11.

- Transition between primary and secondary education.

- Removing barriers to learning identified by the school.

- Targeted support for pupils who are underachieving at school for a variety of reasons, that is, attendance, behaviour and learning.

- Working with families and carers.

- Mainly school based and working within school structures.

- Predominantly time-limited and focused work.

- Mainly full time and work in one school.

- Involved in assessment, target setting and action planning.

Personal Adviser – focus of work

- Emphasis on the 13–19 age group of pupils and young people.

- Transition from year 11 into employment, education and training.

- Provide comprehensive careers guidance for all pupils (universal service).

- Involved in transitional reviews in year 9 for statemented pupils.

- Work with outside agencies and local community groups to support the smooth transition into post-16/alternative curriculum experiences and continuing further education.

- Most work is in more than one school.

- Long-term role working all year round and beyond 16 with young people.

- Outreach work to engage the disengaged.

- Assessment target setting and action planning.

Features of learning mentors and personal advisers

Common features

- Close physical location within a school setting.

- Located in a social inclusion or similar team with the SENCO, LSU manager, EWS, educational psychologist, therapists and range of external agencies.

- Common referral and communication systems, that is, referral forms/protocols, case conferences, access to student data.

- Joint training/staff development activities.

- Joint planning, monitoring and review arrangements.

- Joint initiatives/projects, that is, alternative curriculum packages; group work activities on behaviour, self-esteem and so on.

- Joint home visits and drop-in clinics (self referral, advice and so on).

Complementary features

- Working with individuals and groups of young people.

- The use of a range of assessment tools to identify needs, allocate support, set targets, develop action plans and monitor progression.

- Members of a social inclusion or similar team utilising the full range of skills, knowledge and experiences in order to meet pupils' individual needs.

- Part of a continuum of support for pupils from primary to post-16.

- They can work very effectively in supporting pupils who are in an LSU setting.

Distinctive features

- Personal advisers are employed within a Connexions partnership (either directly, sub contracted or seconded arrangements).

- Learning mentors are employed directly by the school.

- Most personal advisers are line managed by the Connexions team manager but accountable to an identified senior manager within the school.

- Learning mentors are line managed through the school structure.

- Personal adviser emphasis is on the 13–19 age group, including transition post-16, with a limited role in Key Stage 3.

- Many learning mentors' roles have an emphasis on students in years 6–9, including primary/secondary transition.

- Emphasis of the learning mentor is on removing barriers to learning, which will improve attainment and achievement in school.

- Personal advisers have a more holistic/long-term role working all year round enabling pupils and young people to remain engaged with employment, education and training beyond 16.

Supervision

This has become an essential part of working in an Inclusion Team. The process of supervision has been widely used in health and social services, particularly with social workers, nursing therapists and counsellors. A definition of supervision is a support process in which one person is given responsibility to work with another member(s) of staff in order to develop competent and accountable practice.

What are the benefits of supervision?

- Assists managers to have and maintain an overview of current workload.

- Promotes consistency of practice.

- Ensures personal safety and that staff are working within school guidelines or legal framework.

- Challenges practice, which in turn promotes accountability.

- Increases the professional skill base, expertise and raises standards.

- Can help to identify 'dangerous' practitioners and practice.

- Provides a written record of discussion which makes both parties accountable.

How does it support continuing professional development and feedback?

- Identifies professional development needs.

- Focuses on individual career development.

- Identifies where skills and talents are being underutilised, which may in turn affect staff retention.

- Feedback from both parties including the supervisor promotes reflective practitioners.

- Encourages open and honest working relationships.

- Addresses practice issues in a structured way.

For the staff being supervised, it has the following benefits

- Helps develop self-awareness.

- Relieves stress.

- Is a debriefing/offloading forum.

- Helps staff recognise areas of difficulty and sources of support.

- Provides a support structure through periods of difficulty and personal crisis.

In order to ensure that supervision happens in practice, there needs to be the following

- A scheduled time.

- A confidential location.

- A willingness to learn by both parties – no one has all the answers.

- A supervision agreement to prevent misunderstandings.

- Ongoing support/preparation and training for supervisors if they are from within the school – the effectiveness of the whole process will be related to the skills, knowledge and expertise of the supervisor.

Accessing supervisors is another task. This is not about line management, although some aspects can be undertaken in this way. Counsellors and therapists within the Inclusion Team will have the necessary skills; otherwise many schools have 'bought in' services from consultants or professionals. In my view, it is essential to have access to supervision. When the learning mentor strand first started in 1999, it was quickly evident that they were working with pupils with complex problems, and the mentors themselves needed support to help reflect on how they were working with individual cases. Line management is more commonly about outcomes, impact and resources, rather than offering professional debate about cases and how to manage these.

Emerging roles and functions

The emergence of new roles has increased rapidly over the past few years and the remodelling of the workforce agenda has led to more 'non-teaching' roles. Many schools are now appointing 'associate staff/professionals' for positions such as pastoral co-ordinators/managers/team leaders, heads of Key Stages, progress co-ordinators, BEST staff, senior learning mentors, assistant learning mentors, pupil welfare officers and attendance officers, to name just a few. The Inclusion Team is the natural 'home' for these roles. A useful exercise is to look at the *Times Educational Supplement* and other related papers for these emerging roles and apply for job specifications and descriptions. This will ensure that you are keeping up to date with new positions.

In addition, management roles such as curriculum leader for inclusion and assistant headteacher (inclusion) are appearing that require a background in teaching. However, some schools are looking at appointing professionals to these posts who do not have a teaching background. Many are appointing learning support unit managers who have a background in counselling, therapy and other relevant fields, owing to the multi-agency nature of the work. In those schools that are establishing Children's Centres, this background would be a distinct advantage. Those schools that have extended provision would also benefit from staff who are experienced in adult education, out-of-hours work and community provision. Many schools, both primary and secondary, are appointing inclusion managers at assistant headteacher or deputy headteacher level. This represents a significant change from, say, six years ago when there would have been a special educational needs co-ordinator and a few teaching assistants. Inclusion has certainly made its mark here.

In the words of Brian Parker, Headteacher of Longdendale Community Language College, Tameside:

> We've really taken our motto 'We are all here to learn' to heart, with the advent of *Every Child Matters* and the Workforce Remodelling agenda – we are aiming to fulfil our vision by creating posts which go beyond traditional teaching and support roles. The new strategy places a fresh perspective on how we help pupils and their families in overcoming barriers to learning.

Lead professional role

The lead professional role has emerged from *Every Child Matters* in the development of integrated children's services and is included in statutory guidance relating to sections 10 and 11 of the Children

Act 2004. Lead professionals will support those children, young people and families who have additional needs that require input from more than one practitioner. The reason for introducing a lead professional model is to ensure that they secure more coherent, pupil-centred and effective services. This role is much needed within the inclusion agenda. Past experience shows that:

- having too many professionals involved can be confusing for everyone, causes frustration and generates delay in accessing support

- some children fail to get the support of an agency and then 'fall through the net'

- short-term, inconsistent or conflicting support from different professionals can cause loss of trust and confidence in services.

Many existing practitioners could take on this role and the DfES has defined the role in its *Lead Professional Good Practice Guidance*. Examples of such practitioners include personal advisers, health visitors, midwives, youth workers, family workers, nursery nurses, educational welfare officers, school nurses or learning mentors. Hence it is important that schools understand the lead professional role and put in place appropriate support and supervision if one of the Inclusion Team takes on this position.

The lead professional will work with children and young people with a range of 'additional needs' who require an integrated package of support. In addition, those children who have significant or complex needs, such as those who have statements of SEN or are looked after children, may already have a designated practitioner with a legal responsibility; therefore, the role here will be slightly different. More detailed guidance on this will be given by the DfES in the spring term 2006.

The key functions of a lead professional are to:

- build a trusting relationship with the child, young person and family

- ensure the child and family remain central to decisions

- follow up and implement the outcomes of the assessment of the child

- act as a key conduit and contact point for information

- ensure that progress is monitored taking into account the range of needs and circumstances

- ensure that where children, young people and their families require more specialist services, these are effectively co-ordinated and there is a clear exit strategy if required.

It will be important, therefore, that if a member of the team is a 'lead professional' that there is a network of support, training and supervision available. In multi-agency services, line management and supervision arrangements may be split between a practitioner's home agency (that is, the school) and the multi-agency service. A number of local authority areas have appointed 'integrated service managers' to support lead professionals and have introduced a joint assessment framework. These managers may carry out a number of functions, for example, advice and training in delivering the lead professional role, bringing partner agencies on board to deliver the role and resolving difficulties or conflicts between practitioners.

Local authorities, schools and partner agencies should ensure that information-sharing between agencies is properly addressed and that:

- change strategies and service delivery plans incorporate effective and clearly understood mechanisms for sharing information across service and professional boundaries

- relevant managers and practitioners receive adequate training on information-sharing

- managers, practitioners and other staff understand the legal basis on which information can be shared

- sharing information becomes an integral part of the way in which practitioners fulfil their duties

- strategic managers are familiar with the guidance that their managers in Children's Services should follow.

Key workers

Internally, the school may wish to identify a key worker who is responsible for pulling together all support for a particular child. This is up to the school and not the role of the lead professional, which is a statutory, multi-agency function. A key worker can be identified by the Inclusion Panel as the most appropriate person within the school to ensure effective delivery of services for that pupil. The role is accountable to the inclusion manager and inclusion panel.

Recruitment

Recruiting staff is another challenge, particularly for schools which traditionally have recruited mainly teachers or support staff. Also the wide range of needs that are presented by pupils in schools will demand specific types of skills, understanding and knowledge. Therefore the inclusion manager will need to have a range of strategies and scenarios in order to appoint the right person. The CD includes intray exercises that will be useful in recruiting staff to the inclusion team (see the CD, Chapter 4 Example 1).

Advice on recruitment, contractual issues, job specifications and job descriptions can be sought from the local authority or from the school's personnel/human resource section. Again, the scouring of appropriate publications will be useful.

It is important that any recruitment follows the guidelines set out in the *Safeguarding Children – Safe Recruitment and Selection in Education Settings* (DfES, 2005). In addition, risk assessments need to be carried out on all roles in school. These assessments should address the potential risks associated with the role and provide strategies/solutions to avoid them. This is particularly important when working with pupils on a one-to-one basis (where there may be child protection issues), with any work that demands lifting and handling, or working with pupils who have particularly challenging or aggressive behaviours.

Identification and assessment

The early identification and assessment of pupils in difficulty or who have additional needs, is key to the success of the inclusion programme. There needs to be an accurate knowledge base within the school which identifies individuals and groups of pupils who are vulnerable. A variety of tools and assessments can be used around self-assessment, use of academic and curriculum data, specific assessment tools used for basic skills – literacy, numeracy, reading and so on – observations around school, feedback from staff, discussions, specialist teacher/therapist/ support service input and so on. The key to the success of this area and the management of this process is that there needs to be a common framework, understanding and approach agreed by all the professionals working with the pupil. Multi-agency assessment is a challenge. Hopefully the introduction of a 'Common Assessment Framework' and a multi-agency database will make assessment and the access to information a more effective process.

In essence there needs to be a common:

- language around 'assessment' and what it means both within school and with multi-agency teams.

- referral form and subsequent action/improvement planning format to measure progress

- system of recording evidence including minutes of meetings

- database recording support/intervention and outcomes.

Within the Inclusion Team there will be a platform of plans – Individual Education Plan, Personal Support Plan, Looked After Children Plan – the list is endless. Keep it simple – a plan is a plan, and the same format can be used to cover most of the aspects that are required. In the same vein, referral forms will need to be consistent and there should be clear expectations of staff as to the quality and depth of information required for a referral.

It is important for schools to have a common and clear description that is agreed and used by all staff to describe behaviour. Using 'behaviour descriptors' to categorise types and levels of behaviour teacher with the appropriate provision/sanction for that type/level is a helpful way of ensuring that the provision/sanction is appropriate to the behaviour. Many schools who have used this exercise have found that some pupils have escalated up the behaviour sanctions ladder too fast and should have had either another form of sanction or reward. By analysing the pupil's behaviour and applying the appropriate behaviour descriptor, pupils should then receive the most appropriate provision. In many schools, certain groups or individual pupils are 'labelled' as having bad behaviour, but when you actually look at the evidence, it is either not there or is exaggerated because of a lack of objective data.

There is a wealth of information about pupils now available in schools – the challenge is to distinguish what is relevant and what is not; what does it mean and how can we use it to best effect? Often pupils will present an uneven picture when professionals start looking at their behaviour, learning attainment, attitude and so on. Causes of difficulties can be in the home, peers, teacher, curriculum or a mixture of everything. Behaviour descriptors or inclusion indicators are extremely useful in helping to piece together an overall picture of the problem, and of areas of success.

They also can help focus on priorities for allocation of support, and for establishing baselines against which progress can be measured and specific SMART targets can be set. As you can see from the pupil inclusion indicators example, which is also on the CD, Chapter 4 Example 2, there are areas which focus on home/school, self, peers, and classroom practice. Scores can be made in each section and an overall score for inclusion at the end. Classroom practice observations and discussions with appropriate staff will need to be in place to gain accurate data for this exercise. Rotherham Educational Psychology Service has some excellent practice on this issue.

Classroom observations by inclusion staff are an essential element of gathering information, in order to set targets with the pupil and to look at a range of other related areas which may have an impact on attainment and progress. Most teachers will welcome observation and advice or feedback, but the team will have to handle this sensitively and in a positive climate. On the CD, Chapter 4 Example 3 contains a couple of examples of a checklist for observable teacher behaviour and pupil behaviour. The evidence from these can all add to the picture of the pupil and the context within which they are working. Observations in and around the school are particularly important when associated with behaviour or punctuality problems. The Inclusion Team will consist of a number of staff who are not in the classroom full-time and so have a better picture than anyone of who's doing what, where and when, and who's not there at all. The person who checks the registers and 'late book' probably knows more than anyone else. Hence, basic information on pupils can be gathered relatively quickly. However, managers need to note that time does have to be allocated for this when looking at caseloads, as it is an integral part of the identification and assessment process.

Recording, storage and easy retrieval of information is very important. The challenge with inclusion is that there are often too many systems operating, particularly in a large school and, as a result, information disappears or is duplicated several times. In my experience this causes the most frustration. Territorial behaviours start emerging with filing cabinets becoming personal 'comfort blankets'. With information being stored on computer, this unfortunate trait should reduce. If pupil files are still in paper format, they need to include only relevant information, not the life history since birth when the pupil is now 15. It is also helpful to have a checklist sheet at the front with key information (CD, Chapter 4 Example 4). This is born from having spent many sad years in SENCOs' and inclusion managers' filing cabinets.

Administrative support is a key resource which is not negotiable. Although the move is to reduce administrative burdens on staff, the inclusion process in itself generates much information and, together with the statutory requirements of annual review, statementing, SEN tribunals, liaising with a wide number of agencies, minutes of meetings and all the training implications, means that high-quality administrative input is required.

Obviously, it is essential to hold meetings to review progress and assess need; however, there is a tendency to have meetings which are:

- too frequent

- unfocused

- poorly organised and lacking specific outcomes

- not planned as part of regular assess/analyse/plan/act/review process.

Inclusion Teams that have a common template for all meetings find recording information and sharing it easier to handle (see, CD, Chapter 4 Example 5). This template should be filled in and actions agreed as the meeting progresses; this form could then be photocopied and circulated before participants leave. This avoids professionals disagreeing about the outcomes of the same meeting and encourages prompt actions after the meeting. The minutes can then be typed up and circulated formally.

Management of caseloads

Many staff within the Inclusion Team will have a caseload of pupils or, as in the case of an LSU, cohorts of pupils who are identified to enter and exit the provision. Caseloads require careful managing – the tendency for schools that have significant numbers of pupils with barriers to learning is for members of the Inclusion Team to have large and blooming numbers of cases which never reduce. The challenge is to look at caseloads at three levels – those pupils who need:

- significant intervention (daily or several times each week)

- medium intervention (weekly or regular)

- infrequent intervention (monthly or drop-in facility).

The level is allocated according to need and regular reviews of progress move pupils down the list to infrequent intervention. Many pupils just need a drop-in once a week, month or term just to know that support is available, but really do not need to be counted as part of a 'caseload'. In this way staff can 'exit' pupils in a logical and supportive way while enabling other pupils to be taken on. Exiting of pupils is the hardest challenge for both staff and pupils; there can be a tendency for a dependency culture on both sides to be developed. Exit procedures within LSUs, nurture groups or other identified provision need to undertake similar processes. Very rarely will a 'perfect child' (whatever that is) be achieved and there will be degrees of success and a range of coping strategies developed both by the pupil and the school. A real challenge for LSUs are those pupils who have significant behavioural difficulties that require specialist provision; where there is no such provision, these pupils tend to stay in the LSU, which then becomes blocked with pupils who cannot move out either to mainstream classes or to alternative provision. Many schools which have been in this position have created alternative provision for these groups, particularly at Key Stage 4.

Transition

A key role for the Inclusion Team is that of transition. Transition can be defined at varying levels:

- between schools at Key Stages 2 to 3

- mid-term entry pupils – particularly those who move frequently, asylum seekers, and so on

- between classes at the end of the year

- into alternative curriculum/work placement/social groups/college placements and so on

- into LSU/nurture group provision.

Many pupils who have a range of barriers to learning and SEN find change very difficult, and a focus on effective planning for transition, especially between years 6 and 7, is crucial. Where pupils transfer to a mainstream school at times other than the usual transition points, making friends and social contacts can be more difficult, especially for pupils with SEN. The learning mentor role has supported pupils very effectively across this time. Some examples of best practice have included holiday reconnaissance activities at the new school so that pupils are familiar with the territory, and helping pupils to plan their timetable and routes around school. The lack of effective admission and induction arrangements can be a real barrier to inclusion.

The Inclusion Team plays a key role in preparing both pupils and staff to receive pupils with a number of needs. Many schools use the learning support unit and learning mentor support as a 'half way' house to preparing the pupils to enter school. Time invested in this planning is a key to success in the future. The use of LEA support services for pupils with particularly complex needs can be helpful. Resources and training may be available to prepare peers to help understand the complex problems of a 'new member of their community'.

Close liaison with parents at this time is essential to gain their confidence and trust in a partnership that is, hopefully, a lasting one. Again, home–school liaison, learning mentors, educational welfare officers and teaching assistants and specialist teaching staff can all play an important part in this process.

Transition of pupils moving from a LSU or other small group/withdrawal base back into mainstream classes needs to be carefully handled. Planning and preparation of this time is essential to making the process work. There will be failures, but usually this is because the time is not right for either side. A reintegration plan or some kind of agreed action should be in place together with appropriate support and guidance. For some pupils, there is a high degree of dependency on small group work and staff will need to encourage mainstream interaction. Some LSUs and learning bases can create a dependency culture, and some pupils and staff view it as an easy option. Mediation between the receiving teacher and the pupil is often successful in overcoming the initial problems of 're-entry'. Teaching assistants can play a crucial role in ensuring curriculum continuity and effective communication between the key players. Effective communication and time for planning are two very important criteria for success, and managers must plan these into work schedules.

Curriculum – managing access

Schools cater for pupils' curricular needs in a variety of different and flexible ways. There is no blueprint or single model for delivery that is inherently more successful than others. Managers have to balance and match the needs of the pupils with the skills and expertise of the staff. High expectations and high-quality provision must be striven for.

Most pupils will have full access to a broad and balanced curriculum including the National Curriculum. The majority of pupils will be in mainstream classes, with the curriculum tailored to their needs and supported by a range of individual/group support/specialist teaching or withdrawal. Many schools worry about withdrawing pupils from class because they may miss vital information and the school may be criticised by OFSTED. However, pupils will not learn effectively if they are not emotionally comfortable with themselves or their setting, so withdrawal from say Literacy or Numeracy is acceptable as part of a planned and time-limited withdrawal programme if the priority is to resolve or support the pupil's emotional needs. Clearly, there needs to be agreement with the class teacher about the withdrawal programme together with commitment and clear direction from senior managers.

Some secondary schools place pupils in lower sets or bands. The routine placement of pupils in this way can be a barrier to development for some, particularly if these groups become undisciplined, demand attention and make little progress. In many cases these groups can be seen as 'sin bins', whereas in reality they should be the best example of practice in school rather than the worst. Too often pupils are placed because of behavioural difficulties rather than their learning capability.

The Inclusion Team needs to have the resources, skills and ideas to support teachers in delivering a curriculum that is matched to pupils' needs and reduces their barriers to learning. Allocating members of the Inclusion Team to a particular subject area or year group is one approach, having 'link teachers for inclusion' from each department in a secondary school is another. Whatever the approach, time for joint planning, feedback and evaluation is important. Far too often, teaching assistants are not effectively used owing to the lack of time for planning and discussion with teaching staff. Training and collaborative work with specialists must be planned into in-service programmes, professional development targets, peer observations and so on for all staff. Good quality training is essential to make inclusion happen.

Suggestions for making it happen ...

- Good management is about getting the right people and right processes in place to make things happen.

- The Senior Leadership Team and governors need to give clear strategic direction and clout to make it happen. An old Russian proverb about a fish rots from the head down springs to mind.

- Everyone including outside agencies needs to be clear about their roles in making it happen.

- There needs to be understanding of new roles that are emerging, in particular the role of lead professional.

- Be innovative and research best practice elsewhere; check advertisements in the *Times Educational Supplement* (*TES*) and national newspapers for ideas.

- There needs to be a whole-school understanding of differing roles to prevent duplication and tension.

- The recruitment of the right people with a balance of skills, experience and knowledge is essential to meet the current and changing needs of pupils.

- Identification, assessment, transition and curriculum access are key management issues which are high priority.

- Develop a Common Assessment Framework within the context of pupils with SEBD, which in turn should lead to common assessment procedures and protocols for early/ earlier intervention – test out the use of the CAF.

Look it up...

- Belbin – Team Roles, www.belbin.com

- Lead Professional Good Practice Guide, www.everychildmatters.gov.uk/leadprofessional

- Safeguarding Children – Safe Recruitment and Selection in Education Settings, DfES (2005) www.teachernet.gov.uk/childprotection

- Leading and managing change in a multi-agency context, www.ecm.gov.uk/multiagency working/toolkitforteammanagers/managingchange/models/

Self-Evaluation – Measuring the Impact

This chapter looks at how measuring and evaluating the effectiveness and impact of your inclusion strategy and policy is an essential part of making inclusion happen. Self-evaluation is now key to the new OFSTED inspection framework. Shorter inspections will mean a much greater focus on the ability of schools to undertake effective self-evaluation. A range of self-evaluation approaches and tools are considered, and advice is offered on how to complete Self-Evaluation Forms.

Managing self-evaluation

There are many different approaches to self-evaluation and inclusion, with a range of tools, performance indicators and targets available to schools. It is important to adopt a self-evaluation strategy and a range of tools which best fit the nature and context of your school. Self-evaluation is about helping schools ensure continuous improvement and should not be undertaken solely for the purpose of inspection: 'OFSTED recognises the importance of self-evaluation as a continuous process that is complemented from time to time by external inspection' (*Every Child Matters – Framework for the Inspection of Schools in England from September 2005* – OFSTED, 2005).

Self-evaluation needs to be an integral part of the day-to-day management of the school. It should:

- be easily understood and applied across the school

- link clearly into the existing inclusion strategy and policy

- cover all aspects of inclusion in the school including the roles and functions of individual team members

- provide the range of evidence needed to measure performance and progress

- use a range of quantitative and qualitative data, that is, pupils' views, observations, discussions, perceptions as well as statistical numerical data

- be part of an ongoing process linked into whole-school improvement planning

- involve all the 'stakeholders' that is, staff, agencies, parents

- enable easy transfer of evidence into the new OFSTED Self-Evaluation Form (SEF) and the *Every Child Matters* outcomes.

 Figure 5.1 shows a useful PowerPoint presentation for schools and training. This is also on the CD, Chapter 5 Example 1.

Keep it simple. The self-evaluation strategy must be manageable within the school and build on existing effective practices. All too often, self-evaluation or monitoring strategies are imposed on staff with little or no explanation. This can cause resentment and stress, especially if they involve a lot of mindless form filling with little or no discernable outcome. The key questions should be:

- How well are we doing?

- How well should we be doing?

- How do we compare with similar schools?

- What more can we aim to achieve?

- How and what must we do to make it happen?

This has to be a whole-school process linked to school improvement, particularly when in some schools inclusion is seen as the prime responsibility of the Inclusion Team and no one else. Effective whole-school self-evaluation:

- allows a school to focus on improvement where it is most needed

- ensures that the school develops goals that are shared by all staff and tailored to the school's unique character and needs

- empowers the school to articulate what it does well and to collect the evidence to back this up, guard against complacency and develop its own agenda for improvement

- helps the school to plan for effective training that links teacher development with school improvement

- ensures that the school is providing value for money and is using its resources in the best way to raise achievement.

Self-evaluation is best tackled in bite-sized chunks such as:

- how the school is performing against its inclusion strategy

- how it is performing against its inclusion policy

- progress in terms of individual pupils

- progress in terms of groups of pupils

- how the school involves other agencies and the local community to help meet its inclusion agenda.

In this way, the school will be using existing structures and policies which have been contributed to by a range of staff, pupils and agencies, and with which they are familiar. If the inclusion strategy and policy have been thorough and well thought out, the evaluation should fall into

Chapter 5 Example 1 – Powerpoint Slides on Self–Evaluation

Removing Barriers
Developing Inclusive Practice In Our
Schools And Community

Self Evaluation – Making it real....Making it happen!

1

Self–Evaluation

- Audit

- Assessment of need

- Planning for need

- Management systems and structures

- Quality of teaching and learning

- Effective use of support

- Monitoring and evaluation

2

Audit

- What is the current situation?

- SWOT analysis

- Across the whole school

- Involving range of pupils, parents, staff and

  those from range of agencies

3

Assessment of need

- What are the barriers to learning?

- Access to appropriate data?

- Analysis of data?

- Range of strategies to assess

- Communication

4

Planning for need

- Inclusion policies

- Involvement of all staff

- Governor for Inclusion

- Multi-agency approach Every Child Matters

- Multi-agency training

- Early identification

5

Management Systems and Structures

- Inclusion Panels

- Common referal and action planning

- Roles and responsibilities of staff

- Common, complementary and distinctive

6

Quality of teaching and learning

- Inclusive classrooms

- Tracking of vulnerable groups

- Focus on outcomes

- Knowledge and understanding of staff

- Engagement and motivation

7

Effective use of support

- Roles in the classroom

- Learning Mentors

- Learning Support Units

- Service level agreements

8

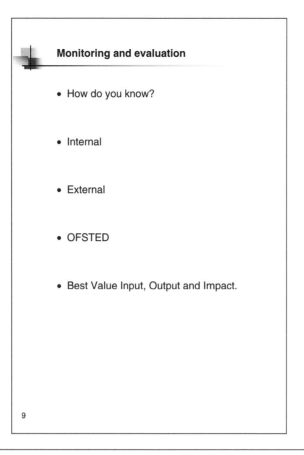

Monitoring and evaluation

- How do you know?

- Internal

- External

- OFSTED

- Best Value Input, Output and Impact.

9

Figure 5.1   PowerPoint presentation on self-evaluation

place as a result. A useful table converting the key statements and outcomes from the strategy and policy can be devised using statements such as:

- in place

- not in place

- predicted OFSTED quality grade.

A full inclusion policy self-evaluation checklist is included on the CD, Chapter 3 Example 3. When this has been completed, it will give a guide as to where the strengths and weaknesses lie. It is at this point that additional audit tools can be used to:

- supplement the evidence and information where it is weak

- make the process more robust and detailed in specific targeted areas

- give guidance and information on best practice in particular areas.

The inclusion strategy and policy will undoubtedly change and develop as the self-evaluation process evolves, however, there are some essential ingredients that will make the process more effective:

- Ensure that inclusion evaluation is:

  - part of the whole school evaluation process to avoid duplication of information and effort

  - part of an ongoing process which is co-ordinated and monitored by an Inclusion Team member

- part of an annual cycle of meetings so information is collected regularly rather than in a rush at the end of year.

- Ensure that staff, pupils, parents and agencies know their roles and responsibilities in the process.

- Specific advisory groups could be established, where appropriate, to oversee the process. These could include members of the governing body, local agencies and community provision.

- Involve the School Council and seek their views at regular intervals. Pupils can carry out surveys and questionnaires which will inform the process.

- Ensure the governing body receives detailed reports and inputs on developments

- Use case studies with staff to show impact. These are particularly useful when pupils are making small steps to improvement and much of the useful and informative data is qualitative rather than quantitative. A useful tip is to create a template for case studies similar to the following:

Case study template

What are the presenting difficulties?

-
-

Areas of strength and success:

-
-

What strategies were put in place?

-
-

What was the impact?

-
-

What are the messages for the pupil?

-
-

What are the messages for the school/agency?

-
-

If this is done on one side of A4 paper and placed on a database, the format can then be used to retrieve information under these headings, which will be very useful in showing impact and those strategies that have been most successful. This could also inform the more effective targeting of resources. The CD Chapter 5 Example 2 is a case study template which can be adapted by schools.

Using data effectively

Using data, whether quantitative or qualitative, is a powerful tool to set benchmarks and measure progress in self-evaluation. The key question for pupils within the inclusion framework is 'has the progress been sufficient?' bearing in mind the particular circumstances of each pupil or groups of pupils. Data can be used to look at:

- how schools compare with others locally and nationally

- improvements over time and within specified time limits

- the progress of different groups of pupils.

Quantitative data is usually associated with attainment, achievement, attendance, behaviour and so on, and is usually easily available in school. In fact, schools are increasingly data rich. The problem is the interpretation of the data and the time to undertake this. I remember on one of my inclusion courses, a participant said 'please don't mention the word data, it makes me feel scared as I was hopeless at maths at school'. This is a problem in some schools owing to the complexity of data systems leading to a 'fear' factor. However, if this is overcome and the Inclusion Team can get 'underneath the data', it is invaluable in setting targets and predictions for individuals and groups of students, which should give a true picture of whether progress is sufficient or not.

There is a range of data available at national, LEA, whole-school, individual and group levels. These include Performance and Assessment (PANDA) data (including value added information), Standardised Assessment Tests and Cognitive Ability Tests, to name but a few.

When measuring individual pupil progress information from a range of plans such as IEPs, PSPs, Behaviour Plans and Looked After Children Plans can be used, together with overall progress in meeting SMART targets. There will be a range of curriculum and personalised targets set with regard to a student's achievement and attainment. These should be realistic, challenging and based on the student's previous and predicted performance.

Group data is particularly important in tracking groups of pupils within the inclusion framework who are underachieving. The new OFSTED Inspection Framework requires that there is evidence of progress and outcomes from specific groups of pupils.

A useful inclusion data package is PASS (Pupils' Attitudes to Self and School), please see their website www.pass-survey.co.uk. It focuses on raising achievement of pupils by recognising their attitudes to:

- feelings about school

- perceived learning capability

- self-regard – long-term learner self-worth

- preparedness for learning – whether learners feel they have the 'tools to do the learning job'

- attitudes to teachers and perceptions of their relationship with school staff

- general work ethics

- confidence in learning

- attitudes to attendance

- response to curriculum demands.

This is useful as it puts qualitative data into a quantitative form enabling these issues to be measured. The results have been extremely informative and the use of this data package has had a positive influence on pupils' attainment, motivation and behaviour, as well as highlighting issues around pupils' mental health. It also helps identify priorities for resources.

With the emergence of multidisciplinary teams, the use of qualitative data in measuring progress has gained importance and credibility. Quantitative data can be enhanced by using qualitative data and hypotheses tested through:

- observations inside and outside the classroom

- discussions with staff, pupils, parents and carers

- perceptions of staff and others

- feelings of staff and others

- video and photographic evidence

- use of school/multi-professional assessments.

By using both quantitative and qualitative data, schools can build up a more informed and whole picture of the pupils.

Existing self-evaluation products

There is no single particular self-evaluation product covering all aspects of inclusion evaluation, and schools will need to use a variety of appropriate tools to assess the impact on inclusion and how well they are serving different groups of pupils. Existing products/tools can be grouped into two key types:

1. Whole-school tools/frameworks which evaluate the overall impact of a school's inclusion approach.

2. Those which evaluate the impact of a specific programme or impact on a particular group of pupils.

Group 1

Within the first group, the following tools are available:

- *Special Educational Needs and Disability – Towards Inclusive Schools* (OFSTED) highlights the issues that schools are facing when including pupils with varying needs, gives practical recommendations and a useful checklist for self-evaluation around pupils' progress, quality of teaching, curriculum, contribution pupils make to the school community and ideas for policy review.

■ *Evaluating Educational Inclusion* (OFSTED) is helpful in setting hypotheses for inspectors to pursue when in a school. Key questions are:

- ■ Do all pupils get a fair deal at school?

- ■ How well does the school recognise and overcome barriers to learning?

- ■ Do the school's values embrace inclusion and does its practice promote it?

- ■ Testing inclusively – questions focusing on educational inclusion to test inspection evidence (www.ofsted.gov.uk).

■ *Quality in Education for All* materials have been developed by Lloyds TSB Bank plc in conjunction with the SEN regional partnerships and are available as a booklet and CD-ROM, free, from the SEN regional partnerships (www.teachernet.gov.uk). The materials contain tools that can be used for self-evaluation in relation to provision for children with SEN and inclusion.

■ The *Index for Inclusion* (Centre for Studies on Inclusive Education) is a well-established framework for self-review and has a range of supporting materials (www.inclusion.org.uk).

■ The *Primary National Strategy* has developed self-evaluation and training tools for inclusion, English as an Additional Language (EAL) and children with special needs.

Many local authorities have developed their own self-evaluation frameworks. For example Manchester has developed *High Standards for All – Manchester Education Department Inclusion Standards* (2004) (www.manchester.gov.uk/education). This has a well developed pack of practical guidelines and checklists.

Group 2

Within the second group, there are a range of tools and audits available.

Behaviour and attendance: in-depth audit for primary schools – emotional health and well-being (DfES)

This is a useful audit aimed at all staff, as well as governors and outside agencies, on leadership and management, whole-school ethos and framework, organisational factors, classroom layout and environment, curriculum delivery, relationships, responses to poor behaviour, pupil support systems, staff development and support. This evidence gives information about culture and values which would be very helpful in an inclusive self-evaluation and support the school's Self-Evaluation Form in the new OFSTED framework (www.dfes.gov.uk/behaviourandattendance). The CD, Chapter 5 Example 3 contains a useful checklist for schools when they are planning to review their behaviour strategy.

Behaviour Audit (DfES)

The behaviour and attendance strategy has a number of good behaviour whole-school audits which have been used by schools in conjunction with the behaviour and attendance consultants.

Learning Mentor Audit Tool (DfES)

This audit tool is designed to help and support schools in their management and implementation of the learning mentor programme. It reflects the DfES good practice guidelines for learning mentors and should therefore support schools in moving towards best practice. It was written by myself and compiled with the help of a team of learning mentor co-ordinators. As with all audit tools, it needs to be completed as a team with a member of the senior management team involved. It covers planning, management, facilities, referrals, systems and documentation, communications within the school and with parents, transition, training and development, monitoring and evaluation, and collecting basic data (www.standards.dfes.gov.uk/learningmentors).

Learning Support Unit Audit Tool (DfES)

Similar to the learning mentor process, this audit tool for LSUs is useful in establishing the role and function of a LSU, and protecting it from becoming a 'sin bin'. Areas of the audit cover policy and whole-school management, perceptions and image, wider involvement and sharing good practice, admission arrangements, reintegration arrangements, routines and organisation, teaching and learning facilities. Again, the results can be used to inform the SEF and the School Improvement Plan (www.standards.dfes.gov.uk/excellence/policies/lsu).

Learning Mentor and Learning Support Units and Supporting School Improvement (DfES)

These two documents have recently been published by the DfES as a self-evaluation framework for LSU managers and learning mentors supporting:

- the five *Every Child Matters* outcomes

- school self-evaluation

- the new OFSTED framework for inspecting schools

- personalised learning.

Learning for All – Standards for Racial Equality (Commission for Racial Equality)

This gives schools an overview of current performance in relation to race issues and strategies to improve their performance.

Changing faces in our schools-meeting the needs of mobile pupils in primary schools (Milton Keynes Council)

This is an excellent folder full of ideas for working with pupils who move frequently. It gives practical examples and guidance for reducing the impact of mobility, raising standards and improving achievement and inter-agency collaboration. It also contains a toolkit of sample documents that can be used in schools as well as case study material. The CD, Chapter 5 Example 4 is the pupil mobility school self-audit framework which schools can adapt to their needs.

The selection of tools and audits will depend on the issues, priorities and context of the school. Research will need to be conducted into which tools are appropriate for which task. This could be a role for particular members of the Inclusion Team and nominated governors.

The OFSTED Inspection Framework 2005

Changes to OFSTED inspections took place from September 2005 – these are set out in the document *Every Child Matters – Framework for the Inspection of Schools in England from September 2005*. Inspections will continue to give a view of the overall quality of the school, what it does well and not so well. There will be, as before, key issues and areas for further improvement. However, there are some key changes, including the following:

- There will be a common set of questions inspectors must ask (known as the *The Common Inspection Schedule for Schools and Other Post-16 Provision*) in every institution or setting providing education and/or training from early childhood to the age of 19.

- Schools will receive very little notice before an inspection.

- Inspections will be short and focused – no more than two days in a school – and will concentrate on working with senior managers in the school.

- The school's self-evaluation evidence will be central to the inspection process. There will be a strong emphasis on how schools use self-evaluation, including regular input from pupils, parents and other stakeholders, to ensure school improvement and for the school's internal planning and development.

- Schools are expected to complete a Self-Evaluation Form which they should keep up to date. This will be downloaded by inspectors prior to the inspection.

The Framework outlines the basis on which inspectors will make their judgements. They will make their judgements in the following key areas:

- *Overall effectiveness* – how effective, efficient and inclusive is the provision of education, integrated care and any extended services in meeting the needs of learners?

- *Achievement and standards* – how well do learners achieve?

- *Personal development and well-being* – how good is the overall personal development and well-being of the learners?

- *The quality of provision* – how effective are teaching and learning in meeting the full range of learners' needs?

- *Leadership and management* – how effective are leadership and management in raising achievement and supporting all learners?

In addition, inspectors will look at the five outcomes of *Every Child Matters* and will consider the following:

- The extent to which schools enable learners to be healthy

- The extent to which providers ensure that learners stay safe

- How well learners enjoy and achieve

- The extent to which learners make a positive contribution

- The extent to which schools enable learners to achieve economic well-being.

There are supplementary questions for all the key inspection judgements and the *Every Child Matters* criteria. The judgement grades are:

- Grade 1 – outstanding

- Grade 2 – good

- Grade 3 – satisfactory

- Grade 4 – inadequate.

Inspectors will use all the evidence gathered through the inspection to arrive at a judgement on the overall effectiveness of the school:

Inspectors are required to arrive at an overall judgement on the effectiveness and efficiency of the school. This judgement should be informed by the judgements inspectors have already made about standards and achievement, the quality of the school's provision and inspectors' evaluation of the quality of leadership and management, in particular the capacity of the school to make improvements and to assess accurately the quality of its own provision. (*Every Child Matters – Framework for the Inspection of Schools in England from September 2005* – OFSTED, 2005)

The Framework also reflects the requirement in the Children Act 2004 for OFSTED to develop (in partnership with others) a coherent framework for the integrated inspection of children's services. This means that judgements made in individual school inspections can feed into the Joint Area Reviews of Children's Services which will be carried out in every local authority area in England over a three-year period. These reviews will evaluate the quality of provision in an area and the extent to which children and young people are achieving the *Every Child Matters* outcomes.

Self-Evaluation Form

The SEF is at the heart of the new inspection arrangements. Schools are expected to complete an SEF which should be kept up to date and added to regularly. The form will summarise the key findings from the school's self-evaluation, identifying weaknesses/gaps together with solutions, and how the school is building on its strengths. The SEF should take clear account of the views of parents and carers, pupils and other stakeholders.

There is no perfect SEF – each SEF will need to reflect the context of the school and its improvement agenda. However, all SEFs should:

- be easy to read and assimilate – bullet points and short sentences are useful

- give a clear picture of how well the school is doing

- provide evidence to back up your judgements/assertions

- show what you are doing to build on successes and improve areas of weakness.

The Office for Standards in Education provides extensive guidance as to how to complete an SEF and schools can log on to its website www.ofsted.gov.uk to complete an interactive form online. There are SEF templates for a variety of schools, for example, nursery, primary, secondary, special, together with guidance on how to complete these. There are also examples of approaches and case studies which schools have used to approach the completion of SEFs. The guidance contained in the document *A New Relationship with Schools: Improving Performance through School Self-Evaluation* (OFSTED, 2004) is particularly helpful. The main headings which should be included in the SEF are as follows:

1. Characteristics of your school

2. Views of learners, parents/carers and other stakeholders

3. Achievement and standards

4. Personal development and well-being

5. The quality of provision

6. Leadership and management

7. Overall effectiveness and efficiency.

For each heading, there are a number of supplementary questions. The range of self-evaluation tools outlined within this chapter will be helpful in providing evidence for the SEF. It is also essential to focus on how your school is meeting the key outcomes of *Every Child Matters*. This can be achieved through considering the questions inspectors will ask around these outcomes and evaluating the findings. The OFSTED SEF templates propose evaluating ECM outcome evidence within section 4, 'Personal Development and Well-being', with the exception of achievement which should be covered in section 3, 'Achievement and Standards'. At the end of each section of the SEF, schools are asked to provide a judgement, using the four OFSTED grades, of how well they think they are doing.

Key points to remember when completing the SEF:

- Ensure you have evidence about the outcomes for different groups of pupils (those identified when identifying the barriers to learning through your audit).

- Inspectors will then expect to see a link between the progress pupils make, the quality of teaching and the effectiveness of leadership and management.

- The clear identification of specific groups of pupils is key, as their progress will reflect the effectiveness of the Inclusion Team and whole school.

- The SEF is an evaluative document and should focus on analysing the impact of what you do, rather than describing it.

- Ensure you understand the key questions in the SEF, be as honest as you can and base your judgements on evidence, not on what you intend to happen in the future.

- The *Every Child Matters* agenda evidence can be elicited from the inclusion policy if it is constructed under those headings, as well as from the inclusion strategy.

School Improvement Partners (SIPs) play an important role in challenging the way the school has undertaken its self-evaluation and the judgements it has reached. They can ask questions, suggest sources of evidence and challenge interpretations of the school's evidence. They are a very useful 'critical friend' in the whole process.

Inspection of Additional Services

Many schools will be developing extended school provision through:

- Children's Centres

- aditional services beyond the school day

- full service Extended Schools.

The Office for Standards in Education will not inspect services which:

- are not directly line managed by the school

- are at an early stage of development

- do not make a direct contribution to the learning and well-being of the children, pupils or students on the school's roll.

However, inspectors will look at the impact of additional services on the *Every Child Matters* outcomes. They will want to discuss:

- why a school has chosen to develop particular services

- what impact the services have on learners, that is, the difference that they make

- how well the school's services are used.

The key focus will be on service provision and impact as a whole, rather than on the inspection of individual services. In the future, some aspects of Extended School services may be inspected through Joint Area Reviews. The Children Act 2004 requires local authorities to co-ordinate all the services provided by statutory, voluntary or private providers for children and young people aged 0–19 as part of an integrated children's service. The *Framework for the Inspection of Children's Services* sets out the principles to be applied in all relevant inspections of services for children and young people. Guidance for these is found in three main documents published by OFSTED (2005):

- *Every Child Matters – Arrangements for Joint Area Reviews of Children's Services*

- *Every Child Matters – Arrangements for the Annual Performance Assessment of Council Children's Services*

- *Every Child Matters – Inspection of Children's Services: Key Judgements and Illustrative Evidence*

The *Every Child Matters* five key outcomes will be the basis for all of the above.

The inspection of pupil referral units will fall under the inspection of schools framework. Most PRUs will be different and will reflect the contextual needs of the local schools and community. The issues and inspection focus, and the range of quality indicators in the SEF will not be significantly different to those applying in all schools. However the following areas are significant for this provision:

- the role, purpose and function of the service/provision

- admission and reintegration arrangements

- the range and quality of the curriculum, behaviour curriculum and outcomes of the pupil

- the costs of the provision in relation to the learning outcomes of the pupils

- key partners and the effectiveness of the relationships – is it just a 'sin bin'?

Any additional services which are part of the PRU such as Child and Adolescent Mental Health Services will not be inspected directly but in future may be part of the Joint Area Reviews.

Self-evaluation is the cornerstone of the new inspection framework and of school improvement. The process of self-evaluation is just as, if not more, important than the final outcome. In previous inspections, schools which have achieved a grade 1 for inclusivity in the 'Summary of the Main Inspection Judgements' have also achieved a grade 1 for quality of the school's links with the community, links with other schools and colleges, the leadership of the headteacher and the value for money provided by the school. In my experience of inspections and working in schools, there is a high correlation between all these aspects of the school's work.

Suggestions for making it happen ...

- Do a trawl of the relevant inclusion data available in the school. Through this process gaps will emerge and areas of focus be prioritised.

- Ensure that there is a full understanding of, and access to, the data held by therapists and others working within the multidisciplinary teams. Some challenges may emerge with regard to confidentiality, which will need to be addressed.

- Set some time aside with a range of key people to discuss the setting of targets.

- The information collated as a result of the above processes must be used to inform the school SEF.

Look it up ...

- Framework for the inspection of children's services, www.ofsted.gov.uk/childrenand youngpeople

- Joint Area Reviews of Children's Services, www.ofsted.gov.uk/childrenandyoungpeople

- Leading on inclusion: Primary National Strategy, www.standards.dfes.gov.uk

- Maximising progress – ensuring the attainment of pupils with SEN www.standards.dfes. gov.uk/keystage3

- Special educational needs and disability – towards inclusive schools, www.ofsted. gov.uk/publications

CHAPTER 6

Maximising Your Resources

This chapter, looks at a range of approaches to ensure the best use of resources in making a real difference to pupils. Another important element of managing the inclusion agenda is ensuring the best use of the resources you have in order to have the maximum impact on pupils. Recent guidance from the government reinforces the requirement for public services to be efficient, effective and secure continuous improvements in performance. With the New Working Relationship with Schools programme, schools will have much greater autonomy and flexibility over how they use their resources, and new methods of procurement are developing.

Best value and efficiency

Best value legislation was introduced in 2000 and places a duty on local authorities to ensure they provide the most appropriate services for their local communities, to make sure that those services are cost effective and competitive, and to deliver year on year improvement in performance. The legislation applies to LAs but not directly to schools. However, the best value principles provide a useful framework for schools and other agencies working in the inclusion field to determine whether they are achieving best practice in their service delivery and its impact on pupils. The concept of best value is not simply about getting value for money. It also considers the quality and impact of service provision through asking the following questions:

■ Should we be delivering this service at all, that is, is it appropriate for our pupils?

■ Can we do things differently?

■ Could someone else deliver the service?

■ Are our services competitive?

■ How do we compare with others in similar positions?

■ How do we consult with customers and stakeholders about the expectations and experiences of the services we offer?

By considering all these issues, schools can determine whether they are offering the most appropriate services to meet the needs of their pupils and whether they are getting best value out of all the resources they use in terms of impact on pupils.

A more recent report *Delivering Efficiency in Local Services* (ODPM, 2004) outlines the government's thrust in ensuring that services provided using public money are efficient, effective and secure continuous improvements in performance. This is known as the Gershon Agenda and is an important element of the government's financial policy. The last Government Spending Review set out clear targets for local government to achieve efficiency gains of at least 2.5 per cent over three years – the government is keen to point out that this is not about saving money per se, or a 'cut' agenda, but more about making better use of public money and putting as many resources as possible into front-line services. Councils which meet or exceed the target can re invest around half the savings made in front-line services or use the money to hold down council tax rises. Overall, local councils are responding positively to the challenge and starting to embed Gershon principles in their organisations.

This agenda applies directly to schools and any other agencies which use public money to provide services. With regard to education and children's social services, the report states that the DfES aims to achieve efficiencies from schools, local authorities and Children's Services.

These will be achieved in a variety of ways – examples include:

- enabling teachers to use their time more productively through workforce reform, which will involve reducing the amount of administration so that teachers can spend more time on teaching and learning, and the recruitment of more highly skilled support staff.

- investment in ICT to enable access to curriculum materials on line, use of interactive whiteboards, computer-based marking and the development of e-learning standards to enable sharing of tools and resources.

In addition, the government aims to improve the procurement of goods, services and new school buildings. The greater devolvement of monies and resources to schools will enable more of the front-line services to go directly to areas of greatest need. Schools will need guidance on more effective procurement of services through partnerships of schools, and Children's Trusts will bring together all relevant local authority services to ensure efficient use of resources. The report states that 'Efficiencies will arise from the creation of extended schools and an increase in the proportion of childcare provision that is schools based and/or children's centre based' (*Delivering Efficiency in Local Services* – ODPM, 2004).

Measuring best value and ensuring the efficient use of resources within the inclusion agenda can be an absolute minefield. However, it is essential that this process is undertaken, for the following reasons:

- The new school funding arrangements from 2006 will combine in one pot a number of grants that were originally ring-fenced for specific programmes.

- As a result of this, the Inclusion Team will have to compete for monies with other areas of the school.

- With the rise in the number of services provided for the wider inclusion agenda, it is essential that they are of high quality and have the maximum impact on pupils.

- The Inclusion Team will probably have the largest budget of the whole school as it will/could include monies for statemented pupils, teaching assistants, learning mentors, learning support units and a range of services such as therapy and counsellors. As a result, the team will need to 'justify' this amount of spend and the impact it makes.

- Pupils' needs are becoming more complex and as a result, additional or different support may be needed. Funds will have to be allocated for this purpose.

- Additional funds may be available through other funding routes and clear rationale and targets will have to be outlined in the bidding/tendering process on how they will improve/develop existing provision and share best practice.

- The Inclusion Team will need financial flexibility to ensure an appropriate response to crisis situations and unforeseen admittance of pupils who have a range of barriers to learning.

On the CD, Chapter 6 Example 1 is a useful framework for senior managers to write a costed action plan for the inclusion agenda.

The government attaches great importance to learning from effective partnership working. A key part of their future policy is the devolution of responsibilities and resources from local authorities to groups of schools and other partners. Hence, within the inclusion agenda, schools will need to have an accurate assessment of:

- how well they use their resources

- how effectively they might share their resources with others, for example, Children's Centres, specialist support staff and so on

- what type of resources they will need.

With the move towards a co-ordinated, multi-professional approach to working with pupils, and the development of childcare and extended services, collaboration with respect to funding and sharing resources are key principles in raising standards and quality. There are a range of possibilities for effective resourcing by these collaborative partnerships of schools. These could include:

- co-ordinated use of specialist schools' community funding

- use of monies from schools which are leading or training schools

- School Sports Partnerships in England can receive substantial funding per partnership to develop sports opportunities

- schools participating in Primary Strategy Networks

- sharing governance structures – such federations can develop streamlined financial decision-making structures across schools. Federated schools which have a joint school company can pool funds to enhance further collaboration.

Further details on such arrangements can be found in the guidance, *Education Improvement Partnerships – Local Collaboration for School Improvement and Better Services* (DfES, 2004).

The DfES guidance on school funding arrangements from 2006–07 refers to the establishment of 'school forums' which will have an important decision-making role as well as their current advisory role. From 2006–07, these local partnerships/forums will have a significant say in the devolvement and distribution of monies in response to local circumstances, together with much greater flexibility. Local Authorities will be required to consult their school forums on the implementation of the new funding arrangements.

Establishing a best value/efficiency model within the inclusion agenda

In my experience, it is important to create a best value/Efficiency model for inclusion which is simple, easy to understand and effective. I have used the following model in schools and training with great success.

Basically the concept is this:

INPUT

Financial, human and physical resources

The range of financial, human and physical resources that are entering the school through various routes and grants. This could also include potential future funding routes, but initially you should include the current ones, that is, SEN funding including pupils with statements; funding from within the school budget for meeting the needs of pupils on School Action and School Action Plus; monies originally from other funding routes such as EiC, BIP, now in the new School Development Grant and so on. Support from other agencies, including LA support services, which are currently predominantly staffing or physical resource based, that is, adaptation and technical aids, support for behaviour, mental health and so on.

OUTPUT

Range of services delivered from the 'INPUT'

Using the available inputs, a range of services will be provided to meet the inclusion agenda. Examples include learning mentors, teaching assistants, LSU staff, Connexions personal advisers, counsellors, the Youth Offending Team, therapists and pastoral support workers.

IMPACT

What effect have the resources and services had on pupils?

As a result of the resources (input) and services provided (output), what is the IMPACT? The criteria for the impact will be determined by the inclusion strategy and policy.

The most common areas of impact will be:

- pupil attainment, achievements, reduction in exclusions, rise in attendance with specific targets

- curriculum access, extra-curricular activities, work-related activities, community activities

- improved links with parents, multi-professional working/networking

- training and development on whole-school ethos, values and quality of provision.

This model provides a very simple way for the inclusion team and managers to ask questions and set hypotheses. For instance:

- Have we got access to and knowledge of the full range of inputs? Are there any additional routes that we could investigate? Could we get more inputs? Where do we find them? Are funds 'lost' in the whole-school budget that should be coming to the Inclusion Team?

- Are the services that we provide in the outputs the services that we need? Do they meet the needs of our pupils? Are they organised/managed in such a way that best value is achieved, that is, referral, communication, contact points? Are they of the right quality and size? Do we have the right number of staff? Do they produce a range of flexible services that meet the needs of staff and pupils – are their skills transferable? How do they complement each other?

- Is the impact what we want? Does it meet/exceed targets? Do certain services have a greater impact on certain areas – do others make little impact? How can we measure the impact on certain pupils, quality of teaching and curriculum? Do we want greater impact in other areas? How can we maximise the impact?

These questions, and there will be many more, will enable the team to:

- audit current provision in targeted areas

- see the correlation between resources, services and impact

- change the input and output if they are not achieving the required impact

- establish clearer priorities in terms of purchasing the kind of resources/services that will have the desired impact

- determine whether the range of services provided are complementary and impact effectively on pupils. If not, this has to be a message for action

- target and monitor resources more effectively

- provide information for a bid for new resources which is based on a clear, simple but effective model that can be understood by everyone

- share practice and debate with others including those from multidisciplinary services.

Practical implications of the model

Input section

If Inclusion Teams are to complete this section effectively, they will require a detailed knowledge of the new funding arrangements for schools. In essence, these are as follows:

- In the future schools will receive a three-year budget. This will enable longer-term planning particularly around staffing and resourcing.

- Local authorities in England will receive a ring-fenced grant from the DfES for their school provision known as the Dedicated Schools Grant (DSG) with a minimum increase of 5 per cent each year. If they wish, local authorities can increase the DSG using other budgets to support *Every Child Matters* work.

- A new School Development Grant (SDG) will bring together a number of existing Standards Funds grants, that is, EiC, Specialist School, BIP, Leading Edge, Training Schools, advanced skills teachers, Gifted and Talented Service Schools.

- Targeted grants will remain separate because they are targeted at specific schools or are time limited. These include Ethnic Minority Achievement Grant, Fresh Start, Primary and Secondary Strategies.

- The Schools Standards Grant (SSG) will provide every school with a direct payment which it can spend as it sees fit.

Access to this information by the Senior Leadership Team will be important. The Inclusion Team will need to ensure that they have knowledge of the amount of funding coming into school and whether it is sufficient to cover the pupils' needs and that of the inclusion provision.

Bidding for more resources from within the school will be a key function of the inclusion manager as will identifying potential external funding routes. Additional funding could come through:

- local partnerships and initiatives

- private sector specific funds

- children's funds

- multidisciplinary funds, that is, those that support health, voluntary agencies and so on, and could be used in a collaborative way

- Learning Skills Council funding emerging out of Strategic Area Review (StAR) reports on students with learning difficulties and/or disabilities

- European funds and so on.

It is important to remember that you should only apply for external funding if it can clearly support your inclusion strategy and policy. Be realistic – if the inclusion provision has to change out of all recognition to access funding, forget it and move on. This is a time-intensive process which needs to have clear outcomes and impact.

If you do decide to apply for funding, the following is a useful approach to constructing a bid.

Who?

- Criteria for eligibility – gender, age, vulnerable groups – is there a clear outlined need?

- Who will take the lead for submission and delivery of the bid – who needs to contribute?

- Will there be a need to recruit more staff, or will there be additional responsibilities for existing staff?

- Are there any training implications?

- Do build in the cost of administration and management.

- Monitoring and evaluation – will this be internal or external or a combination of the two?

- What are the contributions from partners? Get this clear before submitting a bid. Do not assume, as it makes an ASS out of U and ME.

What?

- Be clear about end result/Impact and the range of activities and services/Outputs that will take place to achieve that result.

- Targets should be set and the evidence that will be needed obtained. Targets should be SMART – specific, measurable, achievable, realistic and time limited.

When?

- Deadline for submission – preparation for submission is often time-consuming.

- Information for submission needs to be on a time line.

- All aspects of the bid need to be included in a time plan (grid), including recruitment of staff and so on.

- When will the money become available?

Where?

- Are there transport issues?

- Will there need to be any capital investment to upgrade buildings/develop facilities?

- Are the buildings fit for purpose?

- Is it the right location to serve the individual school and, potentially, the area?

Why?

- Are we doing this? Start from 'what do we want to do and what do we need to do it' rather than 'here is a pot of money and how can we spend it?'

- Use range of statistical evidence using:

  - official statistics

  - published research

- the inclusion strategy and policy and other relevant strategic plans, policies and audits

- action/improvement plans

- government targets and school/area targets.

- Does it fit into school/partnership wider strategy for inclusion?

How?

- If it is a mainstream/Special School bid, how does it improve opportunities for out-reach work and develop stronger links with mainstream schools.

- Does it improve the inclusion of pupils with barriers to learning – does the bid take into account new groups entering the school?

- Does the bid improve multi-agency provision and give a more joined-up service to children and families (including development in health, Children's Services and the voluntary sector)?

- Does the bid improve access within the school? Physical and curriculum access, that is, lifts, ramps, ICT, Braille and so on? What are the implications of the DDA for the school?

- Does it make a real difference to inclusion provision within the school, partnership and local community?

Output section

In terms of looking at practicalities with respect to auditing Output, that is, the range of services which are provided through the Input funding, one key priority will be to establish Service Level Agreements (SLA) with individual service providers. Under an Education Partnership or Federation of Schools, these SLAs may be through the Federation and not with individual schools.

Key headings for a Service Level Agreement could include:

- objectives and targets

- desired outcomes

- core functions

- allocation of support

- range of services

- resources and roles

- access and referral mechanisms

- management responsibilities

- training and development

Cost of provision in year

Year group/ Class group	Activities	Staff services provided	Hours per week	Cost per annum (£)
Year 5/6	One-to-one Individual support	Learning mentors	10 hours	6,000
	Group work/small class support	Teaching assistant	16 hours	4,000
	SEBD service	Support teacher	1 hour	750
	Access to PRU	Transport and time with PRU staff	3 hours	1,500
Total				£12,250
Whole-School Provision				
Administrative time – clerical support				15,000
Resources				25,000
Panel/referral meetings				25,000
Training events including whole-school training				25,000
Staff meetings				3,000
Total				£93,000
				Bristol LA

- data collection and information-sharing

- planning and review

- quality assurance mechanisms – monitoring and evaluation

- minimum requirements from school and agency.

Service Level Agreements should be:

- time limited

- open for review and change in exceptional circumstances

- two sided in terms of what the service can expect from the school, that is access to particular staff, use of telephone, involvement in meetings, as well as what the school can
expect from the service.

A practical way to cost activities/services is to plan out the cost of provision for a particular year
group and/or individual pupils. There is a suggested blank format on the CD, Chapter 6
Example 2, for schools to use and adapt where appropriate, of which a sample is set out below.
Clearly this exercise is easier for a small primary than a large split-site secondary school.

Name of pupil	Year group class	Level of need	Access to services	Level and timing of support	Outcome at 6 week review
Ann Example	Yr 9 9T	School Action Plus Learning/behaviour	Learning mentor PRU Nurture group	2 hrs per week 2 sessions per week Every afternoon	Met targets, no support Continue until summer term Reduce sessions to 3 afternoons, integrate into mainstream classes

This will give the stark reality of the level of service provision and the costings. Schools can break this down further by describing the activities in greater depth. The next step is to look at Impact and then revisit the level of service and cost to see how they complement and correlate with each other.

Impact section

In terms of Impact, a range of data can be used as outlined in Chapter 5 on self-evaluation. Primarily this data will be determined by the framework of the inclusion strategy and policy and the outcomes included within these. In essence, it will be a mixture of quantitative and qualitative data, including the results of questionnaires, views of stakeholders, observations, discussions, pictorial and photographic evidence as well as the impact of training on teacher performance and understanding, better information-sharing, communication with agencies and parents, ethos and values, and so on.

A practical way of bringing together Input, Output and Impact is by the use of inclusion databases. Databases have emerged as an essential part of the Inclusion Team's allocation of resources, deployment of staff and monitoring/tracking of pupil progress and outcomes. With the rise in the number of professionals working within the Inclusion Team, an inclusion database also provides a very useful guide for the inclusion panel as to who is doing what, to whom and when, and to identify gaps and flexibility. A typical database would supersede all other registers such as the SEN register or behaviour register. Many pupils will need access to a range of services, so these registers are almost redundant anyway. The database would have the full range of services available, details of pupils' needs, level of support accessed and outcomes achieved as a result of the service provided. On the CD, Chapter 6 Example 3 is an example of an emerging primary school database.

This information would be updated by administrative staff following the inclusion panel meeting and accessed by all staff. Additional information such as that which is held by key workers or lead professionals could either be added or put in supplementary files with restricted access. The data generated by the inclusion database could be used for a variety of purposes:

- looking at the frequency of particular levels and types of support and their Impact

- planning sufficient time for meetings/reviews and so on

- easy access to information for reports, reviews and so on

- in conjunction with the evidence from the case study database, specific strategies and outcomes can be elicited on individual pupils to look at best practice guidance to share with all staff.

By using the approaches set out in this chapter, schools will be able to ensure that they are accessing the maximum resources to meet the needs of their pupils, that the services they provide are the most appropriate to meet those needs and the use of those resources and services are having the greatest impact on pupils, families and the wider community.

Suggestions for making it happen...

- Knowledge of funding and transparency of budget are two key factors in maximising resources. Managers need to ensure that they have access to all relevant information.

- Governors must be involved in this process and understand the importance of tracking funds and linking this process with impact on attainment and achievement.

- Although inclusion is costly if it is done right, managers and governors needs to recognise that this resource investment will be building capacity within the school and, as a result, is an investment not only for individual pupils, but for the future.

Look it up ...

- Modern Local Government – In Touch with the People; Local Government Act 1999 and a range of other useful information on best value, www.odpm.gov.uk or www.idea-knowledge.gov.uk

- Delivering Efficiency in Local Services 2004, www.odpm.gov.uk

- Education Improvement Partnerships – Local Collaboration for School Improvement and Better Service Delivery (DfES, 2004), www.standards.dfes.gov.uk

- New School Funding Arrangements from 2006–07 (DfES, 2005), www.teachernet.gov.uk/management/schoolfunding

Managing Change Effectively (Without Losing the plot)

The recent developments in education and Children's Services have been introduced at an incredible pace. This can lead to confusion and time spent reading through endless documents without any clear structure. Hopefully, this book will help you in the process of sorting the wood from the trees. In many senses the key issues will be:

- keeping the pupils at the centre of the process at all times

- articulating the inclusion themes, strategy and policy in order that they are fully understood by all staff

- keeping up to date with the changing agenda on an ongoing basis – create a 'favourites' page of the most useful websites and refer to it regularly

- having a common language, without jargon, used by everyone

- communicating like you have never communicated before

- using all staff as change agents – the uniqueness of the multidisciplinary team will mean that they will bring different cultures and a variety of skills

- encouraging risk-taking and innovation

- Keep It Simple … Stupid (the KISS principle).

Managing the change process effectively requires good planning and the ability to maintain an overview at all times and not get too bogged down with the detail. A useful tool in planning the process is force field analysis. This is a process through which driving forces (which can help bring change) and restraining forces (which can hinder it) are identified. From this exercise, priorities can be identified. Restraining forces are usually associated with finance or particular members of staff who have always done it their way. Driving forces could be particular members of staff, hopefully the Senior Leadership Team and governors and pupils.

This exercise would also be useful in providing evidence for the inclusion strategy. The aim is for all staff to understand clearly the reasons for change, to sign up to them so that everyone becomes driving forces. However, it is important to be aware that some staff will resist change for the following reasons:

- insecurity, reluctance to experiment and fear of uncertainty

- how previous changes have been handled … 'It didn't work then, why should it now?'

- misunderstanding of the change and its implications

- uncertainty about how much freedom there is to do things differently

- lack of decision-making skills

- strong peer group pressure

- 'management want change, so therefore resist it'.

This complex area will demand much from the managers of inclusion and they will need to have a range of skills and qualities including:

- leadership and organisational skills

- motivation and drive for achievement

- healthy respect for people and skills in relating to them

- specialist knowledge

- ability to create supportive but risk-taking environments

- being able to look at things holistically and see the 'big picture'

- the capacity not to confront on every issue and a toleration of ambiguity and complexity

- endless enthusiasm.

Find a mentor. All the best leaders and managers have mentors. Someone who will not give you the answers but who can help clarify and crystallise your thinking. It is best if the mentor is outside the school, perhaps even outside education. Use local discussion forums. These will help you acknowledge that there is no simple solution and that other people are finding it just as difficult, or more so, than you are – this always boosts confidence and self-esteem.

At the end of each week, spend a few moments just listing what has been achieved. So often we make lists of what needs to be done not what has been done. Be kind to yourself, allocate time to think and plan. Use wall planners to plot key pressure points over the year so you are prepared. In particular:

- do not attempt to change everything at once; leave a stable and secure base from which new arrangements can be explored

- create formal ways to encourage group and organisational problem-solving

- promote involvement by maximising people's autonomy and participation in the change process

- give adequate time and support to managers and others charged with implementing change

- formalise ways of handling conflict and avoiding Chinese whispers.

Support staff through:

- increasing opportunities at every level to get involved, use their existing skills and learn new ones, and make decisions

- giving them regular time-out for reflection and discussion

- clarifying roles and responsibilities during a period of major change

- considering the use of extra personnel to ease pressure during the transition phase of change

- professional development opportunities and the development of mutual support groups or networks

- ensuring that stress levels are monitored either in management supervision sessions or through mentoring support

- distributing difficult or unrewarding work equitably

- helping staff reduce the stress they often place on themselves by adopting realistic goals.

The most valuable resource a school or agency has is its staff. Without skilled staff pupils will lose faith in services. If the pupil is our client and customer, then they need quality services and resources. By keeping the pupil at the centre of planning and policy, the plot will not be lost and inclusion will happen.

Go for it!

GLOSSARY

ASDAN:	Award Scheme Development and Accreditation Network
BEST:	Behaviour and Education Support Team
BIP:	Behaviour Improvement Programme
CAF:	Common Assessment Framework
CAMHS:	Child and Adolescent Mental Health Services
DDA:	Disability Discrimination Act
DfES:	Department for Education and Skills
DSG:	Dedicated Schools Grant
EAL:	English as an Additional Language
ECM:	*Every Child Matters*
EiC:	Excellence in Cities
EMAG:	Ethnic Minority Achievement Grant
ESPP:	Early Support Pilot Programme
EWO:	education welfare officer
EWS:	Education Welfare Service
FE:	further education
HMI:	Her Majesty's Inspectorate
IAG:	information, advice and guidance
ICT:	information and communications technology
IEP:	Individual Education Plan
JAR:	Joint Area Review
KISS:	Keep It Simple … Stupid!
LA:	local authority
LDD:	learning disabilities and difficulties
LEA:	local education authority
LM:	Learning Mentor
LSU:	learning support unit
NOS:	National Occupational Standards
NRWS:	New Relationship with Schools
NSF:	National Service Framework for Children, Young People and Maternity Services
NVQ:	National Vocational Qualification

ODPM: Office of Deputy Prime Minister

OFSTED: Office for Standards in Education

PANDA: Performance and Assessment

PRU: Pupil Referral Unit

PSP: Personal Support Plan

SDG: School Development Grant

SEAL: Social and Emotional Aspects of Learning

SEBD: Social, Emotional and Behavioural Difficulties

SEF: Self-Evaluation Framework/Form

SEN: special educational needs

SENCO: special educational needs co-ordinator

SENDIST: Special Educational Needs and Disability Tribunal

SIP: School Improvement Partners

SLA: Service Level Agreement

SMART: specific, measurable, achievable, realistic and timely

SSG: Schools Standards Grant

StAR: Strategic Area Review

TOA: Training and Development Agency for Schools

TTA: Teacher Training Agency

UPN   Unique Pupil Number

YISP: Youth Inclusion and Support Panel

YOT: Youth Offending Team

USEFUL BOOKS

Atkinson, Mary, Wilkin, Anne, Stott, Alison, Doherty, Paul, and Kinder, Kay, (2002) *Multi-agency Working: A Detailed Study*, NFER.

Casey, Julie (2002) *Getting It Right: A Behaviour Curriculum*, Lucky Duck Publishing ISBN 1-873942-34-6.

Cowlie, Helen, Boardman, Chrissy, Dawkins, Judith and Jennifer, Dawn (2004) *Emotional Health and Wellbeing – A Practical Guide for Schools*, Paul Chapman Publishing, ISBN 0-7619-4355-2.

DfES (2004) *Commissioning Alternative Provision: The Role of the LEA*, DfES.

DfES (2004) *Guidance for LEAs: PRUs and Alternative Provision*, DfES.

DfES (2004) *National Occupational Standards for Learning Development and Support Services for Children, Young People and Those Who Care for Them*, DfES Publication Department.

DfES (2005) Chaired by Sir Alan Steer, *Report of the Practitioners' Group on School Behaviour and Discipline*, DfES.

DfES (September 2005) *Supporting The New Agenda for Children's Services and Schools – the Role of Learning Mentors and Co-ordinators*, DfES.

DfES (2006) *Working Together to Safeguard Children*, DfES.

OFSTED (2001) *Inspecting New Developments in the Secondary Curriculum – with Guidance on Self-Evaluation*, OFSTED.

OFSTED (2003) *The Education of Pupils with Medical Needs*, OFSTED, HMI 1713.

OFSTED (2004) *A New Relationship with Schools: Improving Performance through School Self-Evaluation*, OFSTED.

OFSTED (September 2005) *Every Child Matters – Framework for the Inspection of Schools in England*, OFSTED.

QCA (2004) *Designing a Personalised Curriculum for Alternative Provision*, QCA.

Wilson, Peter (2004) *Young Minds in our Schools*, Young Minds, ISBN 0-9545123-5-9.

*I*NDEX

Added to a page number 'f' denotes a figure.

A
access 43–4
accountability 10, 45, 68–9
accredited training 61
achievement, inclusion policies 50–1
acronyms 9
additional services, inspection of 98–9
administrative support 80
agency support 22–3
anti-discrimination duties 16
assessment, special needs 8, 20, 78–81
assistant headteachers 76
associate staff/professionals 76
attendance
    aide-memoire 34–7
    see also behaviour and attendance
Attendance Strategy 32–3
Award Scheme Development and Accreditation
        Network (ASDAN) 13

B
barriers to learning 2, 3, 4–5
Behaviour and attendance: in-depth audit for primary
        schools – emotional health and well-being (DfES) 93
behaviour and attendance
    consultants 19
    national programme 19, 62
    training in 62
Behaviour Audit (DfES) 93
behaviour descriptors 79
Behaviour and Education Support Teams (BESTs) 9, 31
Behaviour Improvement Programmes (BIPs) 18, 30–1
behaviour management 19–22
Belbin team worker roles 70, 71
best value 101–3
bidding 106–8

C
caseloads, management 81
Change for Children programme 8
change process, managing 112–14
Changing faces in our schools meeting the needs of
        mobile pupils in primary schools 94–5
Childcare Bill 11
Children Act (2004) 6, 7, 96, 98
Children and Young People Plan 7
children's centres 9, 25
children's services agenda 6–7
Children's Trusts 7
Children's Workforce Strategy 11
Children's Workforce Unit 11
Choice for Parents, the Best Start for Children 11
classroom observations 80
classrooms, inclusive 47–8
code of practice (SEN) 5, 16–17

collaboration, working with behavioural difficulties 30
Common Assessment Framework (CAF) 8, 79
*Common Inspection Schedule for Schools and
        Other Post-16 Provision* 95
Connexions service 13, 38
consultation, strategy development 42
continuing professional development, and supervision 75
costing, activities/services 109
courses, aspiring inclusion workers 60–1
critical friends, governors as 69
curriculum
    access to 43, 82–3
    leaders 76
    strategy development 44

D
data, using effectively 91–2
databases, resource allocation 110
Dedicated Schools Grant (DSG) 10
Delivering Efficiency in Local Services (ODPM) 102
Disability Discrimination Act (2001) 5
Disability Rights Code of Practice for Schools 16
discussion forums 113
displays (classroom) 48

E
Early Support Pilot Programme (ESPP) 24
early years, inclusion agenda 11
economic well-being 52
*Education Improvement Partnerships – Local Collaboration
        for School Improvement and Better Services* (DfES) 103
education service, principles for inclusive 2
efficiency 101–3
*Emotional Health and Well Being – a Practical
        Guide for Schools* 18
enjoyment, inclusion policies 50–1
Evaluating Educational Inclusion (OFSTED) 93
evaluation
    strategy framework 45
    see also self-evaluation
Every Child Matters 6–7, 8, 11, 12, 25, 38, 48–9, 76
Excellence in Cities (EiC) 18, 26, 27
Exclusions Guidance
    Part 1: *Promoting Positive Behaviour and
            Early Intervention* 19
    Part 7: *LEA Responsibility to Provide Full Time
            Education and Re-integrate Permanently
            Excluded Pupils* 21
extended schools 9, 98
Extended Schools Programme 11
external funding 106

F
feedback, and supervision 75
Five-year Strategy for Children and Learners (DfES) 11

funding 3, 10, 39, 103, 105–8
further education agenda 12–13

G
Gershon Agenda 102
governors
    role 68–9
    whole-school training with 62–3
group data 91

H
health, inclusion policies 49
home visits 25

I
identification
    pupils in difficulty 78–81
    in strategy framework 43
impact, best value/efficiency model 104, 110–11
implementation, inclusion strategies 46
Improving Behaviour and Attendance Unit 62
inclusion agenda 1–14
    background to inclusion 1–6
    best value/efficiency models 104–5
    children's services agenda 6–7
    early years 11
    Extended Schools Programme 11
    further education agenda 12–13
    multi-agency working 7–9
    New Relationship with Schools 10
    school workforce remodelling 10–11
    widening 18
    youth green paper 12
inclusion data package 91–2
inclusion indicators 79–80
inclusion managers 13, 67, 113
inclusion models 53–6
    challenges in establishing 57–8
inclusion panels 56–7
inclusion policies 9, 47–53, 89–90
inclusion programmes/initiatives 15–40
    agency support 22–3
    behaviour management 19–22
    funding 3, 39
    selecting and co-ordinating 38
    SEN legislation and framework 15–18
    specific 24–38
    widening inclusion agenda 18
inclusion strategies 9, 41–7, 68, 89–90, 112
inclusion teams 10, 67
    establishing 70
    making the team work 72–4
    plans 79
    pupil support 17
    roles and contributions 71
    template for meetings 80–1
    transitions 81–2
inclusion training 59–64
Inclusive Schooling – Children with Special
    Educational Needs (DfES) 2, 16
inclusive schools 41–66
    inclusion models 53–6
        challenges in establishing 57–8
    inclusion panels and referral process 56–7
    inclusion policies 47–53
    inclusion strategies 41–7
    inclusive training 58–64
    key features 64–6
Index for Inclusion 93
induction 60

information
    about pupils 79–80
    access 44
    recording, storage and retrieval 80
    sharing 7, 8, 77–8
Information Sharing and Assessment Teams 8
input, best value/efficiency model 104, 105–8
inspections
    additional services 98–9
    children's services 8
    see also OFSTED inspection framework
integrated service managers 77
integrated services 9
internal seclusion 21
intervention, strategy framework 43

J
jargon 9
Joint Area Reviews (JARs) 7, 96

K
key milestones, pupils' lives 22
key outcomes 7, 48–9, 95–6
key workers 20, 78

L
language, multi-agency working 9
late books 33, 80
Lead Professional Good Practice Guidance (DfES) 77
lead professional role 76–8
leadership 16, 42
leadership teams 69
learning
    personalised and pupil-centred 7
    strategy framework 44–5
    see also barriers to learning
Learning for All – Standards for Racial Equality (CRE) 94
Learning Mentor Audit Tool (DfES) 94
Learning Mentor and Learning Support Units and
    Supporting School Improvement (DfES) 94
learning mentors 27–30, 33, 73
Learning Skills Council 13
Learning Support Unit Audit Tool (DfES) 94
learning support unit managers 76
learning support units (LSUs) 19, 20, 26–7
local authorities, multi-agency working 7–8, 9
lunchtime clubs 29

M
mainstream colleges 12–13
mainstream education 2, 5, 15
mainstream schools 3, 6
managed-move protocols 20
management 67–84
    caseloads 81
    change process 112–14
    curriculum access 82–3
    emerging roles and functions 76–8
    governing bodies 68–9
    identification and assessment 78–81
    inclusion teams see inclusion teams
    recruitment 78
    senior management/leadership team 69
    strategy framework 45
    structures 10
    supervision 74–6
    transitions 81–2
    see also inclusion managers
mediation 21
mentors 113

monitoring, strategy framework 45
multi-agency panels 8
multi-agency services 77
multi-agency teams 8–9
multi-agency working 7–9

N
National Occupations Standards (NOS) 61–2
National Primary Strategy (DfES) 64, 93
National Service Framework (NSF) 11
National Vocational Qualifications (NVQs) 13, 61
networking 10
New Relationship with Schools 10
A New Relationship with Schools: Improving Performance
    through School Self-Evaluation 97
nurture groups 25

O
observations 80
OFSTED inspection framework 95–6
Open College Network 13
organisation, classrooms 47–8
outcomes
    for children 7, 48–9, 95–6
    strategy implementation 46
output, best value/efficiency model 104, 108–10
outreach support services 5

P
partnerships
    effective resourcing 103
    mainstream and special schools 6
    regional 6
    strategy development 42
PASS (Pupils Attitudes to Self and School) 91–2
Pastoral Support Plans (PSPs) 21
personal advisers 73
personalised learning 7
physical access 43
plans 7, 20, 21, 79
Portage service 25
positive contributions, from schools 51–2
primary schools, inclusion model 54f
Primary National Strategy (DfES) 64, 93
procurement of services 102
professional debate 22
professional development 59–60
protocols, managed-move 20
punctuality 33
pupil inclusion indicators 79–80
pupil management 48
pupil referral units (PRUs) 20, 99
pupil self-referral 55
pupil support 17
Pupil Support (Circular 10/99) 19
pupil-centred learning 7

Q
qualitative data 92
Quality in Education for All 93
quantitative data 91, 92

R
recruitment 78
referrals 20, 22, 55–6
regional partnerships 6
Removing Barriers: A Can-do Attitude (OFSTED) 24
resources 101–11
    best value and efficiency 101–3
    best value/efficiency models 104–5

resources cont.
    practical implications 105–11
    strategy framework 46
restorative justice 21

S
Safeguarding Children – Safe Recruitment and Selection
    in Education Settings (DfES) 78
safety, inclusion policies 49–50
school action/school action plus 16
school forums 103
School Improvement Partners (SIPs) 10
schools
    accessing agency support 22–3
    behaviour management 19–22
    self-evaluation see self-evaluation
    SEN legislation and framework 15–18
    workforce remodelling 10–11
    see also inclusive schools; mainstream schools;
        New Relationship with Schools; special schools
seclusion policies 21, 31
secondary schools
    inclusion model 55f
    'youth offer' 11
self-evaluation 10, 85–100
    frameworks 93
    inspection of additional services 98–9
    managing 85–91
    OFSTED inspection framework 95–6
    Powerpoint presentation 87–9
    products 92–5
    using data effectively 91–2
Self-Evaluation Form (SEF) 96–8
senior management 69
service level agreements (SLAs) 5, 108–9
service provision 9
sin bins 83
Skill Force 32
social and behavioural difficulties 18
Social and Emotional Aspects of Learning
    (SEAL) programme 19
space, management of 48
special educational needs
    assessment 8, 20, 78–81
    government vision for 6
    holistic approach 3
    identifiable 1
    legislation and framework 15–18
Special Educational Needs Code of Practice
    (2002) 3–5, 16–17
special educational needs coordinators (SENCOs) 1
Special Educational Needs and Disability Act (2001) 5, 15
Special Educational Needs and Disability
    Tribunal (SENDIS) 17
Special Educational Needs and Disability – Towards
    Inclusive Schools 1 (OFSTED) 18, 92–3
Special educational needs in the mainstream (OFSTED) 64
special schools 5–6, 38
specialist colleges 13
Specialist Status Programme 38
specialist support services, referrals 20
staff
    benefits of supervision 75
    recruitment 78
    support 114
statementing 5, 17
statements 17–18
strategic planning 42, 67
Strategy for SEN: Removing Barriers to Achievement (DfES) 6
success factors, inclusion strategies 46

supervision 74–6
support
    for pupils 17
    for staff 114
    strategy framework 44
    see also administrative support; agency support;
        learning support units; outreach support services
Sure Start 9, 11, 24–5

T
Tackling it Together – Working Together to Raise
        Attendance 32–3
teaching, strategy framework 44–5
templates
    case studies 90–1
    meetings 80–1
terminology, multi-agency working 9
training
    strategy framework 45
    see also inclusion training

Training and Development Agency for
        Schools (TDA) 62
transition plans 20
transitions 45, 81–2

V
values 16
vision 67

W
wall planners 113
whole-school training 62–4
workforce remodelling, schools 10–11

Y
Youth Inclusion and Support Panels (YISPs) 8
Youth Matters 12
Youth Offending Teams (YOTs) 9
'youth offer' 11